Taylor's Pocket Guide to

Flowering Shrubs

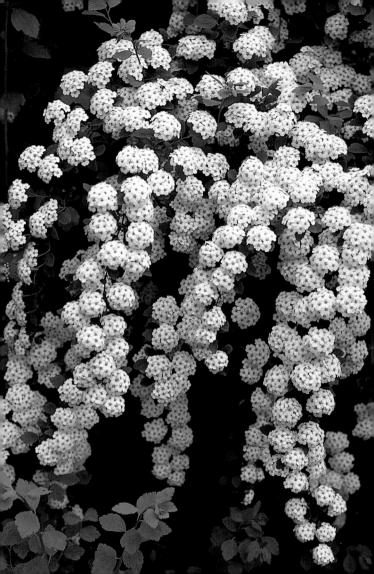

Taylor's Pocket Guide to

Flowering
Shrubs

ANN REILLY
Consulting Editor

A Chanticleer Press Edition

Houghton Mifflin Company

Boston

For information about
permission to reproduce selections from this book,
write to Permissions,
Houghton Mifflin Company, 2 Park Street,
Boston, Massachusetts 02108

Based on Taylor's Encyclopedia of Gardening, Fourth Edition,
Copyright © 1961 by Norman Taylor,
revised and edited by
Gordon P. DeWolf, Jr.

Prepared and produced by Chanticleer Press, New York
Typeset by Dix Type, Inc., Syracuse, New York
Printed and bound by
Dai Nippon, Tokyo, Japan

Library of Congress Catalog Card Number: 89-85030
ISBN: 0-395-52247-1

DNP   10   9   8   7   6   5   4   3   2   1

CONTENTS

Introduction
GARDENING WITH FLOWERING SHRUBS
6

The Plant Descriptions
FLOWERING SHRUBS
25

Appendices
HARDINESS ZONE MAP
106

GARDEN PESTS AND DISEASES
108

GLOSSARY
112

PHOTO CREDITS
121

INDEX
122

GARDENING WITH
FLOWERING SHRUBS

FLOWERING SHRUBS are among the most spectacular members of the plant kingdom, providing a rainbow of color from early spring through late summer. There are golden forsythias, snowy spireas, rich blue hydrangeas, and deep pink azaleas, to list just a few. A shrub always presents a distinctive silhouette in the landscape, whether it be in a hedge or shrub border, a foundation planting, or standing alone in the lawn. Combining practicality with beauty, shrubs can also serve as windbreaks and noise buffers. This book shows you some of the best flowering shrubs for all these uses and tells you how to plant and care for them.

What Is a Shrub?

Shrubs are woody perennial plants that survive for more than two years. There is no strict distinction between trees and shrubs, but plants are usually called shrubs if they are smaller than most trees and have several trunks or stems. Many shrubs, however, grow with only one trunk.

Most shrubs survive winters without dying back, but some die to the ground over winter and produce new stems in spring. Shrubs may be deciduous, evergreen, or semievergreen. Deciduous shrubs shed their leaves each fall, often after providing a display of red, yellow, or orange color. Evergreen shrubs retain their leaves for more than one year. Most flowering evergreens have broad leaves rather than needle-like leaves. Semievergreen shrubs lose some but not all of their leaves over winter. Some shrubs are evergreen when grown in warm areas and semievergreen in cooler areas.

First Steps

The flowering shrubs in this book were chosen because they are both attractive and useful in the landscape. Choosing the right shrub for your yard, and keeping it healthy and colorful, involves assessing your growing conditions and finding a shrub that will thrive in your garden.

Hardiness

A major factor affecting your choice of shrubs is your climate. The ability of a shrub to tolerate cold is called its hardiness. Although hardiness involves other factors, such as soil conditions and availability of water, temperature is the most important factor. The hardiness zone map on pages 106–107 was devised by the U.S. Department of Agriculture to help gardeners determine which plants will grow in their area. The map divides North America into ten zones based on average minimum winter temperatures. Zone 10, with low temperatures of 30° F, is the warmest; zone 1, where the average temperature can drop to −50° F, is the coldest. Locate your area on the map and determine your zone. If you live in zone 5, you will be able to grow most shrubs that are hardy in zones 5 through 1. A shrub hardy to zone 6, however, will probably not survive the winter in your zone unless you have a favorable microclimate.

A microclimate is an area within a zone where conditions differ from the average climate in the rest of the zone; for example, it may be colder on a windy ridge and warmer in a garden enclosed by a wall, fence, or dense hedge. A microclimate can be as large as a lakefront or as small as a backyard garden. Note when your garden blooms in relation to others in your neighborhood. If it blooms earlier, you may have a warm microclimate and may be able to grow plants that won't survive in your neighbors' gardens. If your garden blooms later than others nearby, you may have to grow hardier plants. But before you experiment with microclimates, get to know your garden by growing plants that are known to be hardy in your region.

Although we rate plants according to their fitness to survive cold, many can also be adversely affected by heat. Some shrubs will not produce flower buds unless winter temperatures are cold or freezing. These are identified in the individual plant accounts. Many early-flowering shrubs are hardy in themselves, but their flower buds are vulnerable to late frosts (these are also noted in the plant descriptions). Few flowering shrubs, no matter what their hardiness, can withstand constant strong winds. Study your site before planting. If it is very windy, install a windbreak—a fence, a row of trees, or a hedge of hardy nonflowering shrubs.

Sunlight

Shrubs have varied tolerances for sun and shade. The plant descriptions will tell you the best light conditions for individual shrubs. A shrub that prefers full sun needs at least six hours of direct sun each day. Light or partial shade means four to six hours of direct sun or partially dappled shade all day from taller trees. Shade-loving shrubs should have four hours of sun, or heavily dappled shade all day. No shrub will grow and flower in complete shade, such as the shade cast by tall buildings.

If a shrub is receiving insufficient light, it usually grows lanky, leans in the direction of the strongest light, or does not bloom well. The only way to save it is to increase the light; transplant it or thin out tree branches that shade it.

Soil

Soil is made up of different-sized particles: Clay particles are the smallest; sand particles are the largest; and silt particles fall between the two in size. Clay soils hold water, do not drain well, and become very hard when they dry out. Water drains easily from sandy soils and they dry out quickly. The ideal soil is called loam, with a balance of clay, silt, and sand. If your soil is not ideal, you can easily modify it so that you can grow healthy flowering shrubs.

Organic matter is the main corrective for sand and clay soils. You can use peat moss, compost, leaf mold, dehydrated manure, or other materials. Incorporating organic matter will make clay soils drain better, help sandy soils retain more moisture, activate beneficial organisms in the soil, and supply nutrients. You can also treat clay soil with gypsum (calcium sulfate), which separates individual particles and improves drainage. Most shrubs grow well in average soil, which is about 25 percent organic matter. If a shrub prefers rich soil, that means it needs more than 25 percent organic matter; if it grows best in poor soil, it needs less organic matter.

The Importance of pH

The pH of a soil is the measure of its acidity or alkalinity, rated on a scale of 1 to 14. Neutral soil has a pH of 7, acid soils have a pH lower than 7, and alkaline soils have a pH above 7. The soil's pH affects plants' ability to absorb essential nutrients from the soil.

If you are not sure of your soil's pH, buy a soil test kit at your garden supply store or have the soil tested by your county Cooperative Extension Service or a soil test lab. In general, soils in the East and Northwest are acid, and soils in the Midwest and Southwest are alkaline. If you want to grow a plant that needs a more acid pH than you have, you can lower the pH by adding sulfur. Peat moss and most fertilizers are acid and will also lower pH. To raise the pH—to make acid soil neutral or alkaline—add limestone. Dolomitic limestone is recommended because it does not burn shrub roots and contains the essential element magnesium. It will take several weeks to a month for these elements to correct a soil's pH; incorporate them well before you fertilize and plant.

Fertilizer

Plants need nitrogen, phosphorus, and potassium (potash) to grow, flower, and survive cold. As plants grow, they consume these elements in the soil, and the gardener must replace them with fertilizer. Organic matter does contain some nutrients, but rarely will a shrub do well without additional fertilizer, either organic or chemical. A complete fertilizer contains all three of the essential elements; the three numbers on packages of fertilizer indicate the percentage of each it contains. A package marked 5–10–5 is 5 percent nitrogen, 10 percent phosphate, and 5 percent potash. Look for a fertilizer with a 1:2:1 or 1:2:2 ratio for flowering shrubs because fertilizers too high in nitrogen will encourage lush foliage but few flowers. A good fertilizer for flowering shrubs is 5–10–5.

Phosphorus is essential for root growth but moves very slowly through the soil. Incorporating a high-phosphorus fertilizer such as superphosphate (0–46–0) into the soil at planting time will encourage healthy root growth for many years.

Getting Started

Before you go out and buy a shrub, consider its shape, foliage texture and color, flower color, and mature size. It should complement existing trees and shrubs and your overall landscape design. Some shrubs work well in formal, straight lines and others in informal, free-flowing curves. Evergreens are traditionally used for foundation plantings, especially in front of the home; deciduous flowering shrubs are very effective standing alone and in shrub borders. Low-growing shrubs can be used as tall ground covers and in rock gardens. Dense shrubs and those with thorns can be used as "living fences."

Buying Shrubs

You can buy the shrubs listed in this book at local garden centers or from mail-order nurseries. The advantages to buying shrubs locally are that you can see the plants—both to make sure they are healthy and to decide whether you like their shape, texture, and flower color. Plants bought at garden centers are often larger than those bought from mail-order nurseries. Mail order, however, is a good way to buy unusual shrubs that your garden center may not have.

Planting Shrubs

In deciding when to plant, consider your climate and the type of shrub you are planting. Mail-order nurseries and some local garden centers sell bare-root shrubs, which are dormant shrubs that have no soil around their roots. They must be planted while they are still dormant and without leaves. This can be done in early spring in any climate and in fall in climates with winter temperatures above 10° F. If you plant in fall, do it six to eight weeks before the ground freezes so the roots become established before severe cold.

Shrubs sold in containers or balled and burlapped (with the roots enclosed in soil and held together with burlap) can be planted from early spring until six to eight weeks before the ground freezes. It is perfectly fine to plant these shrubs in summer, but they will need more attention so they do not dry out or suffer from the heat.

How to Plant

Do not attempt to plant shrubs before the soil is ready to be worked in spring. Take a handful of soil and squeeze it; if it remains solid and sticky, it is still too wet. Working it will compact it and ruin its structure. Wait a few days and try again; when it is ready, it will crumble easily. If it is dry and dusty, water it several days before preparing it.

No matter what type of shrub you are planting, you must prepare the soil first. Remove any grass, weeds, or stones, adjust the pH if necessary (two to four weeks before planting), and add superphosphate and organic matter. Mix the soil and the amendments together to a depth of about 2 feet. If you are planting a large area, prepare all the soil in that area. If you are adding only one shrub, prepare the soil in the area of the planting hole.

Specific instructions for planting bare-root, balled-and-bur-lapped, and container shrubs are given below. All types of shrubs should be planted at or very slightly above the level at which they were growing; they will settle a bit as the soil compacts. Make a ring of soil around the shrub at the outer edges of the root spread to hold water. Once the shrub becomes established and starts to grow, the soil can be leveled.

Large shrubs (over several feet high) should be staked at planting time to prevent them from being loosened by the wind. Drive the stake on the windward side of the shrub and secure it with a soft material, but do not tie it tight or the stem will be damaged. Leave the stake in place through one winter.

Bare-Root Shrubs

Never let the roots of bare-root shrubs dry out. As soon as you get them, enclose their roots in wet peat moss or some other material to keep them damp. Store them in a cool, dark place until they can be planted. One day before planting, soak the roots in a bucket of water to restore lost moisture. If any of the roots are damaged, broken, or are much longer than the others, prune them before planting. After preparing the soil, dig a hole wider and deeper than the spread of the roots, and fill the bottom of the hole with a mound of soil for the shrub to rest on that will make its crown level with the top of the ground. Spread the roots out around the soil mound and fill the hole halfway with water; after it drains, fill it to the top with soil and water it again. Prune any broken or damaged branches and remove about one-third of the top growth to encourage root growth.

Balled-and-Burlapped Shrubs

Dig a hole in well-prepared soil twice as wide and deep as the shrub's root ball, then refill the hole with enough soil so the shrub will rest at the right level. Place the wrapped shrub in the hole, cut any strings around the root ball, and loosen the burlap and pull it back slightly, but do not completely remove it. Fill the hole halfway with soil and water it. Let the water drain, then fill the hole completely and water it again.

Container Shrubs

Dig and refill the planting hole in the same way as instructed for planting a balled-and-burlapped shrub. Water the medium in the container and, no matter what it is made of, remove the container. This prevents roots from becoming compacted, which could eventually kill the plant. If the roots are tightly encircling the root ball, loosen them, or cut several slits into the root ball to encourage new root growth. Complete the planting, following the instructions above. If the top growth is extensive and the root ball has been cut, prune back a proportionate amount of the top.

Transplanting

Occasionally, a shrub needs to be transplanted because it is not growing well where it is or because it has outgrown its space. You may need professional help to transplant a large shrub, but you can probably transplant a shrub up to 3 or 4 feet tall yourself.

The best time to transplant is determined by the type of shrub and your climate. Move deciduous shrubs when they are dormant and leafless; transplant them in spring in colder areas (six to eight weeks before summer heat) and in fall in warmer areas (six to eight weeks before the ground freezes). Transplant evergreen shrubs in spring before growth starts or in early fall after the season's growth has matured.

If possible, prune the roots of the shrub several months before transplanting it by cutting into the soil around the roots at the farthest extension of the branches or up to 2 feet across, which is about the heaviest root ball you can easily move. This will encourage a more compact root system. When it is time to transplant, water the shrub first and then dig the root ball from the soil, keeping it as intact as possible. (Deciduous shrubs can be moved bare root, but it is safer to move them with soil.) Have the new planting hole ready so the shrub is out of the ground for only a short amount of time. Plant it in the same way you would a new shrub. After transplanting, cut the top of the shrub back by up to one half, depending on how much of the root system you feel you left behind. Water well after transplanting.

Caring for Newly Planted and Transplanted Shrubs

Because they lack deeply penetrating roots, newly planted and transplanted shrubs are more vulnerable to heat, drought, and wind than established shrubs. After planting, water them often until new growth appears. If the foliage starts to wilt on hot days, spray the leaves with water in addition to deep watering. During the first winter, apply mulch around the plants' crowns and protect the shrubs from winter wind.

Maintaining Shrubs

Once they are established, shrubs require little special attention. You can keep them in peak condition by performing just a few seasonal tasks. It is a good idea to tour your garden once a day so that you become familiar with the plants' growth and can spot any problems before they become serious.

Watering

More shrubs die from lack of water than for any other reason. Most shrubs need 1 inch of water each week, which is best applied to the roots with a soaker hose. If you must water from overhead, do it in the morning so the foliage dries out before night, to help prevent disease. If it is windy or very hot or if foliage wilts, you may need to water more than once a week. Water deeply; frequent light watering encourages shallow roots and can deter a plant's growth or weaken its ability to withstand drought and cold. Water deeply in the fall if it does not rain so the ground is moist when it freezes.

Weeding and Mulching

Weeds compete with shrubs for water and nutrients and are breeding grounds for insects and diseases. Remove all weeds as soon as they appear; most are easily removed when the ground is moist. Be careful when you weed around shallow-rooted shrubs not to disturb the roots. Pre-emergent herbicides, which prevent weed seeds from germinating, can be used safely around shrubs; do not use any other herbicide.

A mulch is a covering spread over the ground and around plants to help reduce weeds and keep the ground moist and the temperature even. Some good organic mulches include bark chips, shredded leaves, and pine needles. Once it is in place, the mulch need not be removed; you can supplement it each year as necessary. Shallow-rooted plants especially need a mulch to keep the roots cool and moist.

Fertilizing

Most shrubs benefit from an annual application of fertilizer. Water the shrub, apply fertilizer to the ground according to package directions, and water it again. Fertilize shrubs in late winter or early spring, before or as growth starts.

Winter Care

All but the hardiest shrubs benefit from special care in winter. Stop fertilizing shrubs in midsummer or early fall, because the nutrients encourage new growth that can be damaged by winter cold. Do not prune late in the season either; pruning also encourages new growth. You can spray broad-leaved evergreens with an antidesiccant in late fall or early winter to keep the leaves from losing moisture. Apply a winter mulch of leaves or pine needles after the first hard frost to plants that are marginally hardy. Some evergreens can be wrapped in burlap to protect them from winter sun and wind, but this is not very attractive.

Pruning

There are many reasons to prune shrubs: to improve their shape, induce new growth and flowers, counteract transplanting shock, keep a plant in scale, and remove dead or dying branches. Depending on your purpose, there are several different pruning techniques.

Pruning Tools

You cannot properly prune your shrubs if you do not have the right tools. Most important are pruning shears; make sure they are sharp, because dull shears can tear rather than cut branches. Don't try to cut any branch that is thicker than the space between the open blades halfway down the blades, or about the thickness of a pencil. For thick branches, use long-handled loping shears or a pruning saw. To shear hedges, use hand-held, long-bladed hedge shears or electric shears.

Pruning Techniques

"Thinning" means cutting out selected branches and twigs to shape or revitalize a shrub. The branches may be cut back slightly or all the way to the ground, depending on how overgrown the shrub is. "Shearing" means cutting all of the branches to shape the plant to a specific form. Whether a shrub should be thinned or sheared depends on its natural growth habit. Compact, twiggy shrubs can be sheared; shearing will make them bushier and neater. Arching, open shrubs should be thinned to maintain their natural form.

The cardinal rule of pruning is to cut back to a branch or node (unless you are cutting the branch to the ground) so as not to leave a stub. Besides being unsightly, stubs left by improper pruning are entry points for diseases.

Timing is critical in pruning flowering shrubs, because pruning at the wrong time can result in loss of flowers. Most spring-flowering shrubs bloom on old wood, which means the buds form on branches that grew during the previous growing season. The right time to prune these shrubs is right after they bloom. Most summer-flowering shrubs bloom on new wood, which means that the buds form on branches that grew in the same year. Prune these shrubs from fall through early spring, before growth starts. (The plant descriptions tell you when to prune each shrub.) Some shrubs die all or part way to the ground over winter. Prune them back in early spring to encourage neat, compact growth. When a large shrub becomes overgrown, the best way to rejuvenate it is to cut one-third of the branches to the ground each winter or early spring for three years. New branches will then grow from the base.

When a row of shrubs is pruned into a more or less formal shape, it is called a hedge; when it is allowed to grow naturally, it is called a shrub border. Plants in a shrub border are pruned the same way as a single shrub. Prune hedges as often as necessary to keep them even and tidy. Be sure that the bottom of the hedge is several inches wider than the top so the lower branches receive light.

Propagation

If you are a beginning gardener, or if you have a new house, you will probably want to buy shrubs at first to form a colorful framework for your house. As your collection increases, you may enjoy propagating new plants from those you already have or from favorite plants of your friends and neighbors.

Cold Frames

Although you can garden without one, a cold frame can make propagating shrubs easier. A cold frame is a bottomless box that is placed on the ground; it has a hinged glass or fiberglass top. A cold frame works like a greenhouse: It keeps young plants warm, protects them from frost, and extends the growing season. When it gets hot during the day, prop the top open; when it cools down at night, close it again.

Cuttings

The simplest way to propagate most shrubs is from softwood cuttings. These are 4- to 6-inch branch tips cut during spring or summer. Remove any flower buds and the lower two or three leaves and place the cutting in a moist medium of peat moss mixed with perlite, vermiculite, or sand. The lower nodes—the scars left when you removed the bottom leaves—must be covered by the medium because the roots will sprout from them. The cuttings may root more quickly if you dust the bases of them with rooting hormone before planting. Cover the container with glass or plastic, place it in light but not full sun, and keep the medium moist. The cutting should root in one to two months. Transplant it into a protected spot or place it in a cold frame over winter before moving it into its permanent position in the garden.

Some shrubs are better propagated from hardwood cuttings (the plant accounts tell you which these are). Hardwood cuttings are 6- to 8-inch branch tips cut in fall as the leaves drop. After removing the lower leaves, slice an inch of bark away from the base of the cutting and dust the wounded base with rooting hormone. Tie a dozen or so cuttings in a bundle and bury them beneath the frost line or place them in a cold frame until spring. During winter, callused tissue forms from which roots will grow later. In spring, dig up, separate, and plant the cuttings upright in a trench, leaving only the top inch of each cutting above ground. Root and top growth will occur; you can transplant the cuttings the next spring.

Layering

Shrubs with trailing or supple branches can be propagated by layering—that is, bending branches to the ground (without breaking them or removing them from the plant) and anchoring them until they root. Scrape the bark from the area to be anchored and coat it with rooting hormone. Secure the branch to the ground with a wire, forked stake, or a brick, and cover the branch with moist peat moss mixed with soil. After the branch roots—it usually takes a year or more—you can cut it from the parent plant and transplant it. The best time to layer is in spring or early summer.

Dividing Shrubs

Some shrubs spread by underground shoots that develop into independent stems, although they remain attached to the parent plant. These stems, with their roots, can be separated from the parent to grow into individual plants. If the plant is small, dig it up and pull the roots apart with your hands or cut them apart with a knife; then plant each piece. Use a sharp spade to sever outer stems from large shrubs, digging deeply to take as many roots as possible. Plant the stems and their root balls as you would any other new shrub.

Seeds

Many species of shrubs can be grown from seeds, but hybrids and cultivars are often sterile or produce inferior plants from seeds. Some shrub seeds have hard shells that should be scarified—nicked or cut—or soaked to make germination easier. Others need a cold period, called stratification, before they will germinate. You can plant these seeds outdoors immediately after gathering them in fall or after storing them for three months in the refrigerator.

Place seeds in pots or in a specifically prepared seed bed that is rich in organic matter. Seeds in pots should be placed in a cold frame over winter. Keep the medium moist during germination and early growth, and transplant the new shrubs after they have several inches of growth. Germination of shrub seeds may be slow; it can take several months after the seeds are stratified, and some seeds may require two stratifications.

A Note on Plant Names

The common, or English, names of plants are often colorful and evocative: Bottlebrush Buckeye, Smoke Tree, Butterfly Bush. Common names vary widely from region to region—Jetbead and White Kerria are both names for the same plant. Sometimes, two very different plants may have the same or similar common names, as with Winter Hazel and Witch Hazel. And some have no common name at all. But every plant, fortunately, is assigned a scientific, or Latin, name that is distinct and unique to that plant. Scientific names are not necessarily more correct, but they are standard around the world and governed by an international set of rules. Therefore, even though scientific names may at first seem difficult or intimidating, they are in the long run a simple and sure way of distinguishing one plant from another.

A scientific name has two parts. The first is called the generic name; it tells us to which genus (plural, genera) a plant belongs. The second part of the name tells us the species. (A species is a kind of plant or animal that is capable of reproducing with members of its kind but is genetically isolated from others. *Homo sapiens* is a species.) Most genera have many species; *Hibiscus,* for example, has more than 250.

Some scientific names have a third part, which may be in italics or written within single quotation marks in roman type. This third part designates a variety or cultivar; some species may have dozens of varieties or cultivars that differ from the species in plant size, plant form, flower size, or flower color. Technically, a variety is a plant that is naturally produced, while a cultivar (short for "cultivated variety") has been created by a plant breeder. For the purposes of the gardener, they may be treated as the same thing.

A hybrid is a plant that is the result of a cross between two genera, two species, or two varieties or cultivars. Sometimes hybrids are given a new scientific name, but they are usually indicated by an × within the scientific name; *Daphne × burkwoodii,* Burkwood Daphne, is a hybrid in this book.

Organization of the Plant Accounts

The plant accounts in this book are arranged alphabetically by scientific name. If you know only the common name of a shrub, refer to the index and turn to the page given.

Some accounts in the book deal with a garden plant at the genus level—because the genus includes many similar species that can be treated in more or less the same way in the garden. In these accounts, only the genus name is given at the top of the page; the name of the species, cultivar, or hybrid pictured is given within the text.

One Last Word

Flowering shrubs can fill your garden with color throughout the spring and summer. From the first forsythias of spring through bright bursts of rhododendrons and waves of deep blue hydrangeas, they can enhance your garden and brighten your landscape all season long. With the basic facts of gardening now at hand, turn to the individual plant accounts that follow to find the shapes and colors that are right for you.

Flowering Shrubs

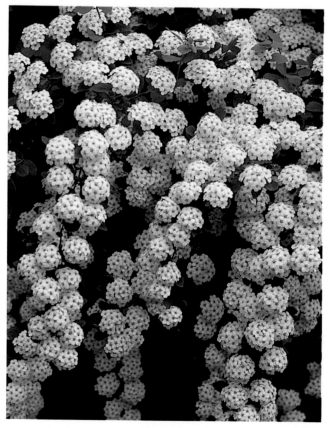

Abelia *(Abelia)*

Glossy Abelia, *A. × grandiflora,* is a graceful, rounded, 3- to 6-foot shrub with arching branches. Clusters of small, fragrant, bell-shaped white or pink flowers bloom from early summer to fall. The 1-inch leaves are bronze when young, shiny dark green in summer, and reddish bronze in fall. Glossy Abelia is evergreen from zone 8 to zone 10 and semievergreen or deciduous in zones 6 to 7. *Abelia* 'Edward Goucher', pictured, grows 4–5 feet tall and has pinkish-lavender blooms. It is hardy to zone 7.

GROWING TIPS

Abelias should be planted in full sun or light shade and fertile, well-drained, acid soil. Prune abelias in early spring before new growth begins. Rejuvenate overgrown shrubs by cutting older branches to the ground in spring. Propagate new plants from stem cuttings or seeds. Abelias can be used as hedges, in foundation plantings, in the shrub border, or standing alone.

Korean Abelialeaf *(Abeliophyllum distichum)*

The arching, spreading branches of Korean Abelialeaf reach 3–5 feet high. In early spring, fragrant white blossoms, star shaped or bell shaped, appear in dense clusters before the foliage opens. Korean Abelialeaf's oval, slightly hairy leaves are deciduous.

GROWING TIPS

Korean Abelialeaf is quite happy in average garden soil, in full sun or in the shade of large trees. Even though the plant is hardy, the flower buds can freeze during cold winters, so plant it in a protected place. Prune immediately after the plant has bloomed; new flowers are produced on the previous year's growth. To encourage new growth, remove older branches to ground level every 2–3 years. Propagate Korean Abelialeaf from softwood cuttings in summer, hardwood cuttings in fall, or from seeds.

Golden Wattle (*Acacia longifolia*)

Golden Wattle is a rapid-growing, free-flowering evergreen shrub or small tree. It reaches 20 feet high and, unlike many other members of the genus *Acacia,* does not have thorns. The graceful blue-green leaves have numerous, narrow, 3- to 6-inch leaflets. The yellow flowers appear in dense, drooping, 2¼-inch spikes in early spring to mid-spring. After the plant has flowered, long, sometimes twisted, seedpods are formed. Golden Wattles make beautiful hedges or specimens but, unfortunately, they are often short-lived.

GROWING TIPS

Plant Golden Wattle in full sun and sandy, well-drained soil. Water it liberally when it is newly planted once it is established, it will tolerate drought. Prune Golden Wattle after it flowers to maintain its shape. Golden Wattle is shallow rooted and should be kept out of high winds, but it will tolerate salt spray. New plants can be grown from semi-hardwood cuttings or from scarified seeds.

Bottlebrush Buckeye *(Aesculus parviflora)*

A member of the horse-chestnut genus, Bottlebrush Buckeye is a deciduous shrub that grows 8–12 feet tall and spreads as wide or wider. White, bell-shaped flowers are produced in cylindrical, 12-inch clusters during the summer. The stamens are pink, prominent, and showy. After flowering, the shrub usually produces egg-shaped nuts typical of the genus.

GROWING TIPS

Bottlebrush Buckeye can be grown in full sun or partial shade in average, well-drained garden soil. Water it deeply during dry periods. It is very handsome standing alone in the lawn or in a border, but it needs plenty of room. Prune it in early spring if needed. Propagate new shrubs by layering or by stratifying seeds.

Running Serviceberry (Amelanchier stolonifera) Zone 4

Running Serviceberry is a slightly sprawling deciduous shrub that grows 3–6 feet high. It spreads by underground stolons and often develops a patchy appearance. The white flowers bloom in early spring in upright clusters; each bloom has 5 petals. The roundish leaves, which open after the flowers, are hairy white on the undersides when they first open. In fall, they turn bright yellow and red. The sweet, purplish-black fruit can be used to make jelly.

GROWING TIPS

Running Serviceberry is easy to grow in full sun or partial shade and average, well-drained garden soil. It tolerates poor soil and grows best where freezing temperatures occur in winter. Prune out older branches in winter or early spring. Propagate Running Serviceberry by dividing the stolons or by stratifying seeds. Serviceberries are alternate hosts for some juniper rust fungi and should not be planted where these diseases are a problem.

Chokeberry *(Aronia)*

Chokeberries are informal deciduous shrubs that bear showy white flowers in ½- to 1½-inch clusters at the ends of the branches in mid-spring to late spring. The flowers' black stamens make an attractive contrast to the white blooms. The small berries that follow have a bitter taste, which accounts for their common name. Red Chokeberry, *A. arbutifolia,* grows 4–8 feet high and has oblong leaves that are gray on the undersides and red in fall. The berries are bright red and last all winter. The hardier Black Chokeberry, *A. melanocarpa* (pictured), grows 2–4 feet tall and has black berries that do not last. Its leaves are shiny and turn red in fall. Because of its lower growth habit, it is sometimes used as a ground cover.

GROWING TIPS

Plant chokeberries in full sun or light shade. They grow easily in a variety of soils and adapt to wet or dry conditions. Thin out crowded branches during the winter. Propagate new shrubs by stratifying seeds or by cuttings or layering.

Groundsel Bush *(Baccharis halimifolia)*

Groundsel Bush is a multi-branched, fast-growing deciduous shrub that reaches 6–12 feet tall. Its gray-green leaves are thick, fleshy, and coarsely toothed. Tiny off-white flowers bloom in dense clusters in summer or fall, followed by thistlelike white fruits. Groundsel Bush is tolerant of salt air and grows as well in the seashore garden as in the shrub border.

GROWING TIPS

Plant Groundsel Bush in full sun and average garden soil. Prune it before growth starts or remove old flower stems after they bloom. New plants may be grown from cuttings or from seeds. Only the female Groundsel Bush produces fruits; if you want the ornamental fruit, plant both a male and a female.

Butterfly Bush *(Buddleia)*

Butterfly bushes attract a profusion of butterflies when their spikes of fragrant, bell-shaped flowers bloom in late summer. Alternate Leaf Butterfly Bush (*B. alternifolia*) grows 10–20 feet tall and has lilac-purple flowers in dense, ¾-inch-long clusters. Orange-eye Butterfly Bush, *B. davidii* (a white-flowered hybrid is pictured), grows 6–10 feet tall. Its flowers, typically lilac colored with an orange throat, bloom in 5- to 12-inch nodding spikes. Butterfly bushes are often called summer lilacs because of their purplish flowers.

GROWING TIPS

Butterfly bushes like full sun and rich, but not heavy, well-drained soil. The tops of plants may die back in winter, but the roots are hardy if they receive protection in the northern limits of the plants' hardiness. Both species are deciduous; prune *B. alternifolia* after it flowers and *B. davidii* either in early spring or after it flowers. Propagate new plants from seeds or from semi-hardwood cuttings taken in fall.

Scotch Heather *(Calluna vulgaris)* Zone 5

Scotch Heather is a shrubby ever-green often grown as a ground cover or a border shrub. It grows 1½–2 feet high and 2–4 feet across. Small bell-shaped flowers bloom in 10-inch spikes in late summer and fall. The flowers are white, pink, or lavender and may be single or double. The variety 'Million' is shown here. The branches of Scotch Heather are covered with fine, scale-like, bright to dark green leaves; the leaves of some varieties turn orange or red in fall and winter.

GROWING TIPS

Plant Scotch Heather in full sun and poor, well-drained, acid soil. Its roots are shallow; apply a mulch to keep them cool and moist and be careful when weeding not to damage them. Prune Scotch Heather in early spring. Provide winter protection in the northern limits of its hardiness. New plants can be grown from cuttings taken in summer. Heather grows well at the seashore and tolerates salt air.

Camellia *(Camellia)*

Camellias are evergreen shrubs prized for their thick, glossy leaves and their waxy flowers of white, pink, or red. Japanese Camellia, *C. japonica,* usually grows 5–12 feet high. Its oval leaves are 3–4 inches long; its flowers, which bloom in winter and spring, are 3–5 inches across. Sasanqua Camellia, *C. sasanqua,* is a loose shrub growing 6–10 feet tall. Its leaves are slender and 2 inches long; its flowers are 2–3 inches across and bloom in fall and winter. The variety 'Showa No Sakae' is seen here.

GROWING TIPS

Plant camellias in partial shade in rich, moist, acid soil with good drainage. Set them in a spot protected from winter sun and wind. Even where the plants are hardy, the flower buds can be destroyed by frost. Mulch in the summer to keep camellias' shallow roots moist and cool and be careful not to damage the roots when you weed. Prune camellias as soon as they have finished flowering. Propagate new plants from stem cuttings or from seeds.

Siberian Pea Shrub *(Caragana arborescens)*

A deciduous shrub, Siberian Pea Shrub can grow 10–20 feet tall but usually grows much lower. The leaves, which are 1–3½ inches long, have 4–6 pairs of leaflets. Yellow pealike flowers bloom close together and give a showy effect in mid-spring to early summer. The plants produce a 2-inch-long seedpod after the flowers have faded. Because of its hardiness, Siberian Pea Shrub is used in cold climates as a windscreen and snow trap. There are dwarf forms that can be used as hedges.

GROWING TIPS

Plant Siberian Pea Shrub in full sun and sandy, well-drained soil. Mature plants will tolerate drought, alkaline soil, and salt. Prune the shrub immediately after it flowers to control the size of the plant and encourage dense growth; cut off the flowers as soon as they fade if you want to prevent seedpods from forming. Propagate Siberian Pea Shrub by sowing seeds that have been soaked in hot water or by rooting stem cuttings.

Bluebeard *(Caryopteris × clandonensis)*

A deciduous shrub, Bluebeard is sometimes called Blue Spirea because the profuse clusters of blue flowers that bloom during the late summer resemble those of the genus *Spiraea*. Bluebeard plants grow 2 feet high and have a mounded shape. The toothed, lance-shaped, 3-inch leaves are aromatic. 'Kew Blue', pictured, and 'Blue Mist' are popular cultivars.

GROWING TIPS

Bluebeard prefers full sun and slightly rich, well-drained garden soil; it tolerates alkaline soil. Water to keep the soil evenly moist at all times. The plants often die to the ground in the colder limits of their hardiness, but the roots will survive if they receive winter protection. In early spring, remove all winter-damaged stems; pruning the plant almost to the ground will result in new, compact, more floriferous growth. Propagate new plants from stem cuttings.

Ceanothus *(Ceanothus)*

Ceanothus, which are sometimes called wild lilacs, are evergreen and deciduous shrubs that bear dense, pyramidal clusters of small blue, white, or lavender flowers in early to late spring. San Diego Ceanothus *(C. cyaneus)*, an evergreen, grows 10–12 feet tall and has 2- to 5-inch clusters of blue flowers. Carmel Creeper, *C. griseus* var. *horizontalis,* is a spreading evergreen 2–3 feet high with 2-inch clusters of blue flowers. Inland Ceanothus, *C. ovatus* (shown), hardiest of the three, grows 2–3 feet high; it has white flowers and red fruits.

GROWING TIPS

Plant ceanothus in full sun and light, dry, well-drained soil. They tolerate slightly alkaline soil and grow well by the seashore. Prune the shrubs after they flower; if they become leggy, cut branches almost to the ground in early spring. Propagate ceanothus from seeds or cuttings, or by layering.

Button Bush *(Cephalanthus occidentalis)*

Button Bush bears globe-shaped, 1-inch clusters of creamy-white, tubular flowers in late summer. The blooms have prominent, decorative pistils. The 2- to 6-inch-long deciduous leaves are heavily veined and are whorled around the stems. Button Bush has a mounded shape and grows 5–12 feet high.

GROWING TIPS

Plant Button Bush in full sun or partial shade. Since it grows naturally in swamps, it prefers constantly moist soil and does best if planted along streams or ponds. The plants need little pruning; when they do, prune back some of the oldest branches to the ground, taking care to maintain the plant's rounded shape. Propagate Button Bush from seeds or cuttings.

Chinese Redbud *(Cercis chinensis)*

In mid-spring, Chinese Redbud bears clusters of rosy-purple, ¾-inch flowers along the branches before the leaves open. The glossy, deciduous leaves are deeply heart-shaped at the base and grow 3–5 inches long. The foliage turns yellow in the fall. Chinese Redbuds grow to 10 feet high.

GROWING TIPS

Plant Chinese Redbud in full sun in open, sandy, well-drained soil. It will not grow well in heavy or constantly moist soil. If the plants become too dense, thin out the oldest branches during the winter. New plants can be grown from scarified seeds, by layering, or from stem cuttings. Chinese Redbud is difficult to transplant once established.

Flowering Quince *(Chaenomeles)*

Flowering quinces are deciduous shrubs bearing single or double, 1- to 2-inch flowers before the leaves open in early spring to mid-spring; these are followed by hard, yellowish fruits that can be used for preserves. Many flowering quinces have spiny branches. Common Flowering Quince, *C. speciosa* (the variety 'Phyllis Moore' is pictured), grows 6–10 feet high. Its toothed, oval leaves are 2–3 inches long; the flowers are pink, white, or scarlet red. Japanese Quince, *C. japonica,* grows 3 feet high and has slightly smaller leaves. Its flowers are brick-red.

GROWING TIPS

Plant flowering quinces in full sun and average, well-drained garden soil. Prune out old branches in early spring and cut back branches that are too long, but do not destroy the shape of the plant. Propagate new plants from semi-hardwood cuttings, root cuttings, or by layering. Quinces are widely used alone or for hedges and in rock gardens.

Rockrose *(Cistus)*

Rockroses are evergreen or semievergreen shrubs with large, 5-petaled flowers that look like single roses. The oval to lance-shaped foliage and the branches are sometimes sticky or hairy. White Rockrose, *C.* × *hybridus*, is a bushy plant that grows 2–4 feet high. Its flowers are 1½ inches wide and white with a yellow eye. Crimson-spot Rockrose, *C. ladanifer* (pictured), grows to 4 feet high. Its flowers, which are fragrant, are white with purple blotches and a yellow eye. Orchid Rockrose, *C.* × *purpureus*, grows 3–4 feet high and has 2- to 3-inch-wide flowers that are reddish purple with a yellow eye and a dark blotch on each petal.

GROWING TIPS

Plant rockroses in full sun and dry, slightly alkaline, well-drained soil. They tolerate drought but not cold, wet winters. If necessary, pinch them back or prune lightly after they flower. Start new plants from seeds or stem cuttings.

Summersweet Clethra *(Clethra alnifolia)*

Also called Sweet Pepperbush or Spiked Alder, Summersweet Clethra has very fragrant flowers that bloom in erect, 5-inch spikes at the ends of the branches in midsummer to late summer. The species has white flowers; the pink-flowered variety 'Pink Spires' is pictured. Summersweet Clethra grows 3–8 feet high. Its oblong deciduous leaves, which are 2½–5 inches long, turn yellow to orange in the fall. The plants are tolerant of seashore conditions.

GROWING TIPS

Plant Summersweet Clethra in full sun or partial shade. It grows best in moist, fertile, slightly acid soil that is well drained. Limit pruning to cutting back old, unproductive branches to the ground in early spring. To start new plants, take cuttings in summer.

Common Bladder Senna *(Colutea arborescens)*   Zone 6

Common Bladder Senna is a deciduous shrub with erect stems that grow 8 feet high. The leaves are divided into 9–13 leaflets. The flowers are bright yellow, pealike, and bloom in spikes from leaf axils in spring and summer. After the plants flower, an inflated, 2½-inch seedpod is formed.

GROWING TIPS

Common Bladder Senna is easy to grow in full sun and average, well-drained soil. It should not be fertilized. After the shrub has flowered, cut it back to keep it neat. Prune Common Bladder Senna in early spring to control its size and shape. Propagate new plants from softwood or hardwood cuttings, by grafting, or from seeds.

Gray Dogwood *(Cornus racemosa)*

One of several dogwood species used in shrub borders, Gray Dogwood grows 8–15 feet high. It has gray twigs and elliptical leaves that are 2–4 inches long and pointed at the tip. The leaves turn bright red to purple in the fall. Small, creamy-white flowers bloom in rounded, 2-inch clusters in early summer. Gray Dogwoods are most effective in late summer, when white berries form on red stalks.

Growing Tips

Gray Dogwood grows in sun or shade and tolerates both wet and dry soil conditions. The plants are very dense and can be used as barrier plants. They take well to shearing. Rejuvenate overgrown plants by cutting a third of their branches to the ground each year for 3 years. To grow new plants, root hardwood stem cuttings in summer.

Winter Hazel *(Corylopsis)*

Blooming in early spring at the same time as forsythia, winter hazel is an equally dazzling, but neater, shrub. Its tiny yellow flowers bloom in nodding clusters before the leaves open. Fragrant Winter Hazel, *C. glabrescens,* grows 8–15 feet high. It has egg-shaped, 4-inch-long leaves and fragrant, ½-inch flowers. Buttercup Winter Hazel, *C. pauciflora* (pictured), grows 6 feet tall and has oval, 2- to 3-inch leaves. Its ¾-inch-long flowers are cup shaped.

GROWING TIPS

Plant winter hazel in full sun or light shade in sandy, slightly acid, well-drained soil. It needs little pruning; shape the plants after they have bloomed. Propagate winter hazel from softwood cuttings in summer, leaving the cuttings undisturbed until growth starts the following spring. Flower buds and flowers may be killed by late frosts in northern areas.

Smoke Tree *(Cotinus coggygria)*

Smoke Tree, or Smokebush, is a deciduous shrub that grows 10–15 feet tall. Its oval, 2- to 3-inch leaves turn red in the fall; there are varieties with purple leaves. The small yellowish flowers, which bloom in large-branching clusters at the ends of the branches, are not very showy. Smoke Tree received its common name from the smoky effect of the masses of pink, gray, or purple fruiting panicles; they are covered with long, spreading hairs and appear in summer with and after the flowers. These clusters are 7–10 inches long.

GROWING TIPS

Plant Smoke Tree in full sun and average, well-drained soil that is not too rich. Young plants are difficult to transplant and need a lot of attention and frequent watering; when they mature they need little care. Prune Smoke Tree lightly, if necessary, when it is dormant. New plants can be grown by stratifying seeds, which grow rather slowly, or from softwood cuttings.

Cotoneaster *(Cotoneaster)*

Cotoneasters are a large group of shrubs that have small white flowers in the spring and showy black or red berries in fall. Creeping Cotoneaster, *C. adpressus,* grows 1–1½ feet high, and has deciduous leaves, pinkish flowers, and red berries. Cranberry Cotoneaster, *C. apiculatus,* is a semievergreen growing 3 feet high, with pink flowers and scarlet berries. Bearberry Cotoneaster, *C. dammeri,* is a 12- to 18-inch evergreen with white flowers and red fruit. The variety 'Skogsholm' is seen here. Spreading Cotoneaster,

C. divaricatus, is a deciduous, upright shrub, 3–7 feet tall, with pink flowers and red berries.

Growing Tips

Cotoneasters prefer full sun but will tolerate partial shade. They grow best in soil that is well drained and neutral to slightly acid. Once established, the plants tolerate drought and wind. Prune in winter or spring only if the plants need shaping or to control their size. Grow new plants from cuttings or by layering.

Scotch Broom *(Cytisus scoparius)*

Zone 6

Although it is deciduous, Scotch Broom appears to be evergreen because its dense branches remain green all winter. The plants, which grow quickly to 4–9 feet high, have tiny leaves that cling closely to the thin branches. The flowers, which bloom profusely in mid-spring, are pealike, bright yellow, and 1 inch long. There are varieties with pale yellow, red, and yellow and red flowers; 'Goldfinch' is pictured. Warminster Broom, *C. × praecox,* and Easter Broom, *C. racemosus,* are related, but less hardy, species.

GROWING TIPS

Scotch Broom likes a spot in full sun and poor, slightly acid to neutral soil that is well drained. Scotch Broom will withstand drought; let the soil dry out between waterings. After the plant has flowered, prune it to keep it compact. Mature plants are difficult to transplant. New plants can be started from cuttings or from seeds.

Daphne (*Daphne*)

Daphnes are grown for their pretty, fragrant clusters of early-spring flowers. Burkwood Daphne, *D.* × *burkwoodii*, is a semi-evergreen shrub that grows 4 feet high. Its flowers are pink, fading to white, and bloom in 2-inch clusters. The variety 'Somerset' is shown here. Rose Daphne, *D. cneorum*, which grows 12 inches tall, has 1½-inch clusters of pink flowers. Fragrant, or Winter, Daphne, *D. odora*, grows 4 feet high. Its flowers are rosy-purple and bloom in 1-inch clusters.

GROWING TIPS

Plant daphnes in full sun or light shade and loose, sandy, neutral to slightly alkaline soil that has excellent drainage. They should be planted out of afternoon sun and should not be over-watered. They benefit from mulches in summer and winter and protection from winter sun and wind. Prune daphnes after they flower. Grow new plants from cuttings, by layering, or by stratifying seeds.

Deutzia *(Deutzia)*

Deutzias are deciduous shrubs that bear clusters of small, star-shaped flowers in late spring. Slender Deutzia, *D. gracilis,* grows 2–5 feet high and has slightly shredding, yellowish-gray bark. The narrow, oblong leaves are 1½–2½ inches long; the flowers are white and single. Fuzzy Deutzia, *D. scabra,* is a branching, arching shrub that grows to 8 feet high and has red-brown, shredding bark. The hairy, oval leaves are 3 inches long. The white flowers, sometimes pink-tinged, may be single or double. The variety 'Candidissima' is shown.

GROWING TIPS

Deutzia will grow in full sun or partial shade in any well-drained garden soil. Prune out any twiggy growth in early spring; if the plant needs shaping, prune it after it flowers. New plants can be grown easily from softwood cuttings.

Leatherwood *(Dirca palustris)*

Zone 5

Years ago, the branches of Leatherwood, or Rope Bark, were used to tie things together, hence its common names. Leatherwood is a tough-wooded, pliable, deciduous shrub that grows 3–5 feet high. The yellow flowers bloom in early spring before the leaves open. The ½-inch flowers have no petals but have a petal-like calyx and bloom in small clusters in the axils of the previous year's wood. The dark green, elliptical leaves grow 2–3 inches long.

GROWING TIPS

Plant Leatherwood in shade; the foliage will fade if it receives too much sun. It needs moist, well-drained soil; if the soil is dry, enrich it with organic matter. Prune Leatherwood after it flowers if necessary. The bark contains a substance that can cause skin irritation, so handle Leatherwood with care. Propagate new plants from seeds or by layering.

Redvein Enkianthus *(Enkianthus campanulatus)* Zone 5

Redvein Enkianthus is a deciduous shrub that grows up to 12 feet high. Its 1- to 3-inch leaves turn brilliant red in the fall. The bell-shaped, ½-inch flowers, which are veined with red, are white to pale yellow and often have pink tips. They bloom in drooping clusters in mid-spring. The tiny, oblong or egg-shaped seedpods that follow are green at first, later turning rusty brown.

GROWING TIPS

Plant Redvein Enkianthus in full sun or partial shade, in rich, acid, well-drained soil. Choose its permanent home carefully because it does not transplant well. It is not showy from a distance, so plant it near the house. Redvein Enkianthus needs pruning only to shape or thin out old branches; prune after the shrub has flowered. New plants can be grown from cuttings or seeds.

Darley Heath *(Erica × darleyensis)*

Darley Heath has tiny, pink, urn-shaped flowers that bloom in showy, 3- to 6-inch clusters in winter and early spring. A low evergreen shrub, Darley Heath grows 2 feet high. Its tiny, needle-like leaves are densely crowded along the branches. The edges of the leaves are rolled.

GROWING TIPS

Like all heaths, Darley Heath prefers full sun or partial shade and rich, moist, well-drained soil. Darley Heath grows best in acid soil but will tolerate neutral to slightly alkaline soil. Protect it from drying winds, especially in winter. Apply a summer mulch to keep the shallow roots cool and moist, and fertilize little if at all. Prune Darley Heath in spring after the flowers have faded. Increase plants from seeds or softwood cuttings.

Pearlbush *(Exochorda)*

Two species of pearlbush are commonly grown in the garden; both bear white flowers in mid-spring to late spring. Common Pearlbush, *E. racemosa,* has arching branches that grow to 15 feet high. The flowers are 2 inches across and bloom in dense clusters of 6–10 flowers. *E. × macrantha* 'The Bride', pictured, is a dwarf variety that grows 4 feet high. Its flowers are larger and more numerous than those of *E. racemosa.*

GROWING TIPS

Grow pearlbush in full sun to partial shade and well-drained, slightly acid soil. Prune plants after they have flowered, removing weak branches from the inside of the plant and trimming as necessary. Start new plants from seeds, layering, or softwood cuttings.

Forsythia *(Forsythia)*

Forsythia's 4-petaled yellow flowers, which prettily clothe the plants before the leaves open, are favorite harbingers of spring. Border Forsythia, *F. × intermedia* (pictured), grows 10 feet high and has somewhat arching and spreading branches. The oblong to oval leaves are toothed and 3–5 inches long. The flowers are 1½ inches across. Weeping Forsythia, *F. suspensa* var. *sieboldii*, grows to 12 feet high and has widely arching branches that may touch the ground. The leaves are like Border Forsythia's; the flowers are smaller and less numerous.

GROWING TIPS

Plant forsythia in full sun or partial shade and any well-drained garden soil. They can be sheared but are more effective when left to grow naturally. Prune to shape them and control their size after flowering. Rejuvenate overgrown shrubs by cutting a third of the branches to ground level. New plants are easily grown from cuttings or suckers.

Dwarf Fothergilla *(Fothergilla gardenii)*

Dwarf Fothergilla's fragrant white flowers bloom in oblong, 1-inch spikes before the leaves open in mid-spring. The flowers have no petals but have numerous white stamens, which give them a fluffy appearance. This deciduous shrub grows 3 feet high and has 1- to 2-inch-long leaves that are dark green on the upper surfaces and bluish white and hairy on the undersides; they turn orange to red in fall. A larger species, *F. major,* has the same type of flowers but grows 4–10 feet high.

GROWING TIPS
Fothergillas grow best in full sun and sandy, well-drained, acid soil. They need little pruning; remove the oldest branches every few years. Propagate fothergillas by softwood cuttings taken in summer or by stratifying seeds.

Gardenia *(Gardenia jasminoides)*

Gardenia, or Cape Jasmine, is an evergreen shrub prized for its rich fragrance. Its waxy, white, 3½-inch flowers are semidouble or double; they bloom in spring and summer. The glossy lance-shaped leaves are 2–4 inches long. The species grows 2–5 feet high; some cultivars grow to 8 feet high.

GROWING TIPS

Grow Gardenias in full sun in cool areas and partial shade where summers are hot. They grow best in soil that is moist, acid, rich, and well drained, in a spot protected from drying winds. Be careful when you weed not to damage the shallow roots; protect them with a mulch. Fertilize Gardenias monthly during their growing period. They grow and flower best where days are hot and humid and nights are below 65° F. In areas where they are not hardy, they may be grown in containers. If the leaves turn yellow, check the soil's acidity and apply iron chelate if necessary. Prune Gardenias after they flower to thin, shape, and remove weak wood. Grow new plants from softwood cuttings.

Box Huckleberry *(Gaylussacia brachycera)*

Box Huckleberry's flowers and berries are similar to those of its relatives in the blueberry family. The tiny, bell-shaped flowers, which are white or pink, bloom in clusters in mid-spring. The fleshy berries are blue but are not as tasty as blueberries. Box Huckleberry (or Juniper Berry) grows 6–16 inches high and spreads by underground stems. Its erect branches are densely covered with elliptic, bright green leaves that are 1–1½ inches long and evergreen.

GROWING TIPS
Box Huckleberry grows best in partial shade; in full sun the foliage turns reddish. Soil should be moist, acid, and well drained. Box Huckleberries need little pruning; when necessary, prune in early spring. Propagate new plants from seeds, by layering or division, or from semi-hardwood cuttings.

Woodwaxen *(Genista)*

Woodwaxens, also commonly known as broom, are low-growing, often evergreen shrubs with green bark and profuse clusters of yellow or white flowers. Lydia Woodwaxen, *G. lydia,* pictured, is a spreading shrub that grows 2 feet tall and blooms in summer. It is useful as a ground cover. Dyer's Greenweed, *G. tinctoria,* is an upright shrub, growing 3 feet tall. Its yellow flowers, which bloom in mid-spring, are used in dye.

Growing Tips

Woodwaxen prefers full sun and dry, well-drained, either acid or alkaline soil. Woodwaxen does not transplant well, so choose its location with care. Prune it after the flowers fade to trim and shape only; heavy pruning may deter the plant's growth. It needs no fertilizing. New plants can be started from cuttings, seeds, or by layering.

A sure sign of the end of winter is the appearance of the fragrant yellow flowers of witch hazel, which open before the leaves. Hybrid Witch Hazel, *H. × intermedia,* grows to 20 feet high. Its round to oval, 3- to 4-inch leaves turn yellow to red in fall. It is hardy to zone 5. Chinese Witch Hazel, *H. mollis,* (the variety 'Brevipetala' is pictured), grows to 15 feet high and has round, 3- to 6-inch leaves that are finely toothed and hairy. Its golden-yellow flowers are reddish at the base. It is hardy to zone 6. Common Witch Hazel, *H. virginiana,* grows 20 feet high and has elliptic, 4- to 6-inch leaves that are coarsely toothed. It blooms in the fall and is hardy to zone 4.

GROWING TIPS

Witch hazels are easy to grow in sun or shade and ordinary garden soil, although they prefer moist soil. Prune witch hazel after it flowers only if it needs thinning or shaping. Propagate plants from seeds, which take 2 years to germinate, or from softwood cuttings.

Rose-of-Sharon (*Hibiscus syriacus*)

Rose-of-Sharon blooms in mid-summer to late summer when few other shrubs produce color. The funnel-shaped flowers are single or double and 3–5 inches wide. They may be red, pink, purple, or white, and usually have a contrasting eye. The variety 'Althea' is pictured. Rose-of-Sharon grows 5–15 feet tall and has oval, 2- to 5-inch-long leaves that are sharply toothed.

GROWING TIPS

Rose-of-Sharon tolerates a wide range of light conditions from full sun to full shade. It will grow in any garden soil that has good drainage; it prefers rich, moist soil but tolerates poor soil and drought. If it is left unpruned, Rose-of-Sharon grows like a small tree; pruned, it can be quite bushy. If you choose to prune, do it in spring as the leaves open. Propagate Rose-of-Sharon from seeds or softwood cuttings made in summer. New plants grow easily from dropped seeds.

Cream Bush *(Holodiscus discolor)*

A spreading, deciduous shrub, Cream Bush grows from 3–20 feet high and has graceful arching branches. Its toothed, oval leaves, which grow 2–4 inches long, are white and felty on the undersides. Showy, feathery, 9-inch-long flower clusters made up of numerous tiny creamy-white flowers appear in summer.

GROWING TIPS

Cream Bush prefers full sun and open, dry, sandy soil that is well drained. It is difficult to transplant, so choose its location with care. The plants self-seed easily; remove the flowers as they fade to prevent this. Prune Cream Bush in spring or after it flowers to keep it neat. New plants can be grown from seeds or by layering.

Hydrangea *(Hydrangea)*

Hydrangeas are grown for their showy summer blossoms. Smooth Hydrangea, *H. arborescens,* is an open, 3- to 5-foot plant. Its white flowers appear in flat to round, 2- to 5-inch clusters. Bigleaf Hydrangea, *H. macrophylla,* has round, 6- to 10-inch clusters of pink or blue flowers. Panicle Hydrangea, *H. paniculata* (the cultivar 'Grandiflora' is pictured), grows 8–20 feet high. It has 8- to 12-inch clusters of white flowers. Oakleaf Hydrangea, *H. quercifolia,* grows 6 feet high and has white flowers in 10-inch panicles. All are deciduous.

GROWING TIPS

Plant hydrangeas in partial shade and rich, moist, well-drained soil. Bigleaf Hydrangea will have pink flowers if grown in neutral to slightly alkaline soil that is high in phosphorus and blue flowers in acid soil low in phosphorus. Prune Oakleaf and Bigleaf hydrangeas in fall. Smooth and Panicle in spring. Do not prune out new shoots of Bigleaf Hydrangea. Propagate hydrangeas by softwood cuttings in summer.

St. Johnswort *(Hypericum)*

St. Johnsworts are grown for their showy yellow flowers, which have prominent stamens and bloom in summer. Aaronsbeard St. Johnswort, *H. calycinum,* is a deciduous or evergreen shrub, depending on the climate, that grows 12–18 inches high. The oblong leaves are 3–4 inches long; they turn purplish in fall. The flowers are 2 inches across. Golden St. Johnswort, *H. frondosum,* pictured, grows 4 feet high and has blue-green, deciduous leaves that are 2–3 inches long. The flowers are 1–2 inches wide.

GROWING TIPS

Grow St. Johnswort in full sun or partial shade. It is not fussy about soil and will tolerate sandy, alkaline, and dry soil. Prune St. Johnswort severely to shape it and control its size in early spring; cut overgrown plants to the ground. Propagate new plants by softwood or hardwood cuttings, by division, or from seeds.

Virginia Sweet Spire *(Itea virginica)*   Zone 5

Virginia Sweet Spire is a deciduous shrub grown for its summer bloom and rich red fall color. It grows 5–10 feet high and has slender, upright branches that are reddish when young. The oval leaves are narrow and 2–4 inches long. The fragrant white flowers bloom in upright or drooping, 6-inch-long clusters.

GROWING TIPS

Grow Virginia Sweet Spire in sun or shade and moist, well-drained soil. Little pruning is needed; it should be done in early spring only to shape the plant and remove dead wood. Propagate new plants by rooting stem cuttings taken early in the summer.

Winter Jasmine (*Jasminum nudiflorum*)

Few shrubs have as long a blooming period as Winter Jasmine. The ¾- to 1-inch, fragrant yellow flowers open in late winter before the leaves and remain for 2 months or more. The plant grows 4–5 feet high and has stiff, arching, angled branches, which can be trained to grow over a wall. The leaves are dark green and have 3 oval leaflets, each 1 inch long.

GROWING TIPS

Winter Jasmine can be grown in full sun or partial shade; more flowers are produced when it is grown in the sun. It grows best in dry, well-drained soil. Prune back as needed after the flowers fade. Propagate Winter Jasmine by layering, by rooting semi-hardwood cuttings, or from seeds.

Laurel *(Kalmia)*

There are 2 laurels, both with evergreen leaves. Mountain Laurel, *K. latifolia* (pictured), is a rounded shrub growing 7–15 feet high. The rose to white flowers bloom in 4- to 6-inch clusters in early summer. Sheep Laurel, *K. angustifolia,* works best in a wild planting. It has a thin, open, spreading habit and grows 2–3 feet high. The lavender-rose flowers bloom in spring in 2- to 3-inch clusters. The stamens of both species curl back and are attached to the petals.

GROWING TIPS

Laurels prefer partial shade and moist, rich, acid soil. Winter sun will burn the leaves. If the leaves turn yellow, check the soil's acidity and apply iron chelate if necessary. Mulch to protect the roots and keep the soil cool and moist. Prune laurels after the flowers fade. Propagate new plants by seeds; Sheep Laurel can also be grown from hardwood cuttings.

Japanese Kerria *(Kerria japonica)*

Japanese Kerria is grown for its attractive golden-yellow flowers and slender green stems. It grows 4–6 feet high and has long, arching branches and bright green, deciduous leaves that are deeply toothed and prominently veined. The flowers, which have 5 petals and are ¾–1½ inches across, bloom in midspring to late spring. The cultivar 'Pleniflora', pictured, is larger and more vigorous than the species and has double, globe-shaped flowers.

GROWING TIPS

Japanese Kerria is very tolerant of shade and of poor soil as long as it is well drained. Thin out dense growth every few years and cut the plants back if necessary after they flower. Propagate new plants by division or from cuttings. Japanese Kerria is useful in shrub borders and foundation plantings.

Beauty Bush *(Kolkwitzia amabilis)* Zone 5

Cultivated for its showy bloom, Beauty Bush is a deciduous shrub that grows 6–12 feet high in an upright, arching, and spreading habit. The leaves are oval and grow 2–3 inches long. There is a variety with variegated leaves. Five-petaled flowers bloom along the branches in late spring and early summer; they are single, trumpet shaped, and pink with a yellow throat. The mature stems usually have peeling reddish bark.

GROWING TIPS

Beauty Bush grows equally well in full sun or partial shade. It will also grow in any type of well-drained soil. Give it a spot where it can spread out. The plants can become twiggy; prune out old wood in early spring. Other pruning should be done after the plant has flowered. Propagate Beauty Bush by softwood cuttings or from seeds.

Leucothoe *(Leucothoe)*

Two leucothoes are grown in shrub borders and evergreen foundation plantings for their attractive, lance-shaped leaves, which turn red or bronze in winter, and their graceful, fragrant, urn-shaped flowers, which bloom in mid-spring to late spring. Coast Leucothoe, *L. axillaris* (pictured), grows to 5 feet high and has arching branches. The flowers are white and bloom in drooping, 1- to 2-inch clusters. Drooping Leucothoe, *L. fontanesiana,* grows 6 feet high and has slender, arching branches and white flowers in 3-inch clusters.

GROWING TIPS

Leucothoes grow best in partial to full shade but will tolerate full sun if the soil is kept constantly moist. They prefer moist, acid, extra-rich soil that is sandy and well drained. Prune leucothoe after it flowers to shape the plant; cut old stems to ground level. Propagate new plants by division, cuttings, or seeds.

Privet (*Ligustrum*)

Privets, which are grown for hedges, have small, white, tubular flowers that appear in clusters in early summer. Amur, or Hedge, Privet, *L. amurense,* is deciduous and erect, growing to 15 feet high. The oval leaves are 1½–2½ inches long. Japanese Privet, *L. japonicum,* is an evergreen that grows 7–10 feet high. The leathery leaves are oblong to oval and 3–4 inches long. Border Privet, *L. obtusifolium,* is a spreading or arching shrub that grows 8–12 feet high. The oblong leaves are deciduous and grow 1½–2½ inches long. Regel's Privet, *L. o.* var. *regelianum,* shown here, is lower and has horizontally spreading branches.

GROWING TIPS

Privet is easy to grow in full sun or partial shade and adapts to any soil condition except constant wetness. The plants grow fast and are not difficult to transplant. You can shear them at any time but if you prune in early spring, flowers will not form. Grow new plants from seeds or softwood or hardwood cuttings.

Tatarian Honeysuckle *(Lonicera tatarica)*

The commonest of the bush honeysuckles and the easiest to grow, Tatarian Honeysuckle grows 8–10 feet high in a vigorous, upright habit. The deciduous leaves are oval to oblong and grow 1–2½ inches long. Small, fragrant, white to deep pink flowers bloom along the branches in mid-spring. Red berries form in the fall. Winter Honeysuckle, *L. fragrantissima,* has fragrant white flowers in late winter and early spring; Amur Honeysuckle, *L. maackii,* is a large, spreading plant that blooms in mid-spring to late spring.

GROWING TIPS

Tatarian Honeysuckle will grow in full sun to full shade in any garden soil, although moist soil is best. Because its growth is quite dense and twiggy and old growth quickly dies back, Tatarian Honeysuckle requires heavy pruning every year. Prune before, during, or immediately after it flowers. New plants can be propagated from stem cuttings or from seeds.

Loropetalum *(Loropetalum chinense)* Zone 7

Loropetalum is closely related to the witch hazels and has similar, but showier, flowers. The 1-inch blooms, which are creamy white and fragrant, appear in early spring. The neat, 6- to 12-foot plants are clothed in oval, 1- to 2-inch leaves.

GROWING TIPS

Loropetalum will grow in either sun or shade. It prefers extra-rich, acid soil that is moist and well drained. Loropetalum will withstand severe pruning but is more attractive if left to grow in its naturally round shape. It can be trained to grow against or over a wall. Propagate by taking cuttings in midsummer and treating them with rooting hormone, or by grafting.

Lily Magnolia *(Magnolia quinquepeta)*

Lily Magnolia is a large, spreading, deciduous shrub that grows to 12 feet high. Its hairy flower buds open into lily- to tulip-shaped, slightly fragrant, 4-inch flowers with 6 petals. The flowers are white on the inside and pinkish purple on the outside; they bloom in mid-spring before the leaves open. The leaves, which are oval and 3–7 inches long, are light green and soft and hairy on the undersides when they first open.

GROWING TIPS

Lily Magnolia prefers full sun but will tolerate light shade. It grows best in deeply prepared, extra-rich, acid soil that is moist and well drained. All magnolias have a fleshy root system that is close to the surface, so be careful when working around the roots. Prune in spring after the flowers fade only if necessary to shape or remove dead wood. Prune out suckers if they develop. Propagate magnolias from seeds or softwood cuttings taken in summer.

Star Magnolia *(Magnolia stellata)*

A spreading shrub or small tree with many branches, Star Magnolia grows to 15 feet high. Its young growth is soft and hairy. The flowers, which appear before the leaves in early spring, are white and fragrant, measuring 3 inches across. They have numerous narrow petals that curl with age. The broadly oval to oblong, 1½- to 5-inch-long leaves are dark green above and light green underneath.

GROWING TIPS

Star Magnolia prefers full sun but tolerates light shade. Like all magnolias, it grows best in very rich, moist, acid soil with good drainage. Plant it in a protected area where late spring frosts will not damage the flower buds. Magnolias do not transplant well; if necessary, transplant magnolias very carefully in spring with a large root ball. Prune in spring after the flowers fade to shape, control size, or remove dead wood. Propagate new plants from softwood cuttings taken in summer, or from seeds.

Mahonia *(Mahonia)*

Mahonias are evergreen shrubs grown for their spiny, glossy green leaves, which turn red to purple in fall. Tiny, fragrant, urn-shaped flowers bloom in midspring, followed in fall by edible, blue to purple berries that resemble grapes. Oregon Grape Holly, *M. aquifolium,* pictured, grows 3–6 feet high. The flowers are yellow and bloom in dense, 3-inch clusters. Leatherleaf Mahonia, *M. bealei,* grows 6–12 feet high. The lemon-yellow flowers bloom in upright, 4-to 6-inch clusters.

GROWING TIPS

Mahonias grow best in partial shade with protection from wind and winter sun, which can burn the leaves. They like rich, moist, acid soil that is well drained. If branches become long and leggy, prune them in spring before growth starts. Pinch new shoots back to keep plants compact. Mahonias are propagated from softwood or hardwood cuttings or from seeds.

Oleander *(Nerium oleander)*

Oleanders are evergreen shrubs or small trees that grow 8–20 feet high. The narrow, leathery leaves, which are 4–10 inches long, are dark green above and paler green underneath. The fragrant, 2½-inch flowers bloom in clusters at the tops of the plants' many branches in spring and summer. They may be yellow, red, white, pink, or purple. Some cultivars have double flowers. All parts of this plant are highly toxic and should be handled with great care.

GROWING TIPS

Oleander must be grown in full sun in a hot location. It grows in any well-drained soil and tolerates heat, drought, slight alkalinity, sandy soil, and salt air. Prune Oleander in early spring to size and shape it. Propagate Oleander from softwood cuttings taken in summer; handle cuttings with care and wash your hands after working with them. New plants can also be grown from seeds.

Holly Osmanthus, a slow-growing evergreen shrub, can reach 20 feet high but is usually much lower. It has stiff, glossy, holly-like leaves that are 1½–2½ inches long. Fragrant white flowers bloom in 1- to 1½-inch clusters in fall. The variety 'Myrtifolius' is shown here. Fortune's Osmanthus, *O. × fortunei,* a fragrant shrub that can grow to 20 feet, and Fragrant Tea Olive, *O. fragrans,* which is highly fragrant and grows to 25 feet, are related species.

GROWING TIPS

Plant Holly Osmanthus in partial to full shade; other *Osmanthus* species prefer partial shade. *Osmanthus* grow best in rich, moist, acid soil with good drainage. They are tolerant of heavy pruning and can be clipped into hedges. Grow new plants from semi-hardwood cuttings taken in late summer.

Common Mock-Orange
(*Philadelphus coronarius*)

Zone 5

Common Mock-Orange, also sometimes called Sweet Mock-Orange, is a deciduous shrub that grows to 10 feet high and wide. The bark is dark brown and peeling; the pointed, ovalish leaves are 1½–4 inches long. Creamy white, highly fragrant flowers, which may be single or double, bloom in clusters at the ends of the branches in late spring. Lemoine Mock-Orange, *P. × lemoinei,* grows 4–6 feet high and has very fragrant flowers. Virginal Mock-Orange, *P. × virginalis,* a 5- to 10-foot shrub, has less fragrant, semidouble or double flowers.

GROWING TIPS
Mock-oranges prefer full sun but will grow well in partial shade. They grow in any well-drained soil and tolerate dry soil. They tend to become leggy and need annual pruning after the flowers fade. Grow new plants from semi-hardwood cuttings taken in summer, by layering, from suckers, or from seeds.

Jerusalem Sage *(Phlomis fruticosa)*

A small, many-branched shrub, Jerusalem Sage is somewhat coarse in appearance. It is a deciduous plant that grows 2–4 feet high. Its stems are covered with yellow matted hairs; its wrinkled, oval leaves are gray-green and grow to 4 inches long. The yellow, 2-lipped flowers bloom in rounded whorls in early summer.

GROWING TIPS

Jerusalem Sage grows best in full sun and dry, infertile, well-drained soil. If you remove the flowers as soon as they fade, Jerusalem Sage will bloom a second time. In fall, cut the plant back by a third to shape it and keep it compact. Propagate new plants from seeds or cuttings or by dividing the roots.

Common Ninebark (*Physocarpus opulifolius*)

A very hardy, deciduous, erect or arching shrub, Common Ninebark has shreddy or peeling bark, which gives it its common name. Ninebark grows 5–10 feet high; it has oval to round, 3-lobed leaves that grow 2–3 inches long. Dense, 2-inch clusters of small white flowers tinged in pink appear in late spring. They are followed by small, inflated, red to brown pods in clusters of 5. The leaves of the variety 'Luteus', Goldleaf Ninebark, are yellow when they open—they look like flowers from a distance—and change to green in summer.

GROWING TIPS

Common Ninebark grows well in sun or shade and average garden soil and tolerates drought. Pinch plants when they are young to encourage bushy growth. If you prune ninebark after it flowers you will not have seedpods; prune instead in winter. Remove old wood to the base to encourage new growth. Propagate from softwood or hardwood cuttings, by division, or from seeds.

Pieris *(Pieris)*

Pierises (sometimes called andromedas) are evergreen shrubs, grown for the clusters of white to pink, urn-shaped flowers that appear in early spring and for their oblong, dark green leaves, which are reddish when they first appear. Mountain Pieris, *P. floribunda,* grows 3–6 feet high; the leaves are 1½–3½ inches long. The fragrant, nodding flowers bloom in upright, 2- to 4-inch clusters. Japanese Pieris, *P. japonica,* grows 3–10 feet high. Its slightly fragrant flowers bloom in drooping, 3- to 5-inch clusters. *P. j.* 'Wada' is shown.

Growing Tips

Pierises prefer partial shade and grow best when they are protected from afternoon and winter sun. They like rich, slightly acid, moist soil that is well drained. Apply a mulch in summer to protect the roots and keep the soil cool and moist. Prune pierises to shape them after they flower. Propagate new plants by layering or from seeds. Japanese Pieris roots easily, but Mountain Pieris is more difficult to root.

Trifoliate Orange *(Poncirus trifoliata)*

Trifoliate Orange, sometimes called Hardy Orange, is a close relative of the *Citrus* genus. It is a large shrub or small tree that grows 6–20 feet high. The leaves, which have 3 oval or oblong leaflets, each 2–3 inches long, are deciduous. Its white, usually fragrant flowers, which have 5 petals and grow 2 inches across, bloom in mid-spring. The 2-inch orange fruits that form in fall are very showy. They have a strong citrus aroma but are bitter and are best used for preserves.

GROWING TIPS

Trifoliate Orange likes a spot in full sun and well-drained, acid soil. You can let it grow naturally or shear it into hedges; it has large, sharp thorns and can be used as a barrier plant. Start new plants from seeds or by taking softwood or hardwood cuttings.

Shrubby Cinquefoil *(Potentilla fruticosa)*

Shrubby Cinquefoil is a small, spreading, multibranched deciduous shrub that grows 1–4 feet high. Its single bright yellow flowers bloom in showy, 1- to 1½-inch clusters in late spring through summer. There are also varieties with white, red, and pink flowers. Each leaf has 3–7 tiny, lance-shaped leaflets, which are rolled at the margins and covered with short, silky hairs.

GROWING TIPS

Shrubby Cinquefoil prefers full sun and fertile, dry soil. It tolerates heavy and alkaline soils as well as drought. Cut the plants back by a third in winter to keep them compact. Start new plants from softwood cuttings.

Dwarf Flowering Almond
(Prunus glandulosa)

Dwarf Flowering Almond is a member of a large genus of ornamental trees and shrubs that includes the flowering almonds, peaches, plums, and cherries, as well as the fruiting species. It is a showy, deciduous shrub that grows to 5 feet high and has slender, erect branches. The oval to oblong leaves are toothed and 1½–4 inches long. Numerous ½-inch flowers bloom along the branches before the leaves unfold. They are white or pink and may be single or double.

GROWING TIPS
Plant Dwarf Flowering Almond in full sun and fertile, sandy, well-drained soil. Prune it after it flowers if necessary to shape the shrub or control its size. Propagate new plants from cuttings.

Exbury Hybrid Azalea
(*Rhododendron* Exbury)

Zone 5

All azaleas belong to the genus *Rhododendron*. Most *Rhododendron*s are evergreen, but some, such as the Exbury Hybrids, are deciduous. Exbury Hybrid Azaleas grow 4 feet high and have oblong leaves that turn yellow, red, and orange in fall. The flowers, which appear in early spring in 3-inch clusters, may be yellow, pink, cream, orange, red, or rose; the variety 'Aurora' is pictured.

GROWING TIPS
Plant azaleas in full sun to partial shade and rich, moist, acid soil that is well drained. Apply a mulch to keep the roots cool and moist and to protect them. Be very careful when working the soil not to disturb the roots. If the leaves turn yellow, check the soil pH; apply iron chelate to improve acidity. *Rhododendron*s do not grow well in areas where winter temperatures are above freezing. Prune azaleas to shape and size them in spring after the flowers fade. Hybrid plants should be propagated from softwood cuttings.

Yako Rhododendron
(Rhododendron yakusimanum)

Yako Rhododendrons are used for foundation plantings and as specimens. They are evergreen and grow 3 feet high in a compact, rounded shape. The oblong, 3-inch leaves are white and densely hairy beneath. The flowers are bell shaped, white or pink, and 2½ inches wide. They bloom in late spring in 6- to 10-inch clusters at the ends of the branches.

GROWING TIPS

Plant rhododendrons in partial shade and rich, acid soil that is moist and well drained. Protect the shallow roots with a mulch, and protect the plants from drying winds. Remove flower clusters as they fade but be careful not to disturb the new shoots, which grow from the base of the flowers. If necessary, prune after flowering. The leaves of rhododendrons naturally curl under when freezing temperatures occur. Increase plants from softwood cuttings; species will also grow true from seeds.

Jetbead *(Rhodotypos scandens)*

A neat deciduous shrub, Jetbead, or White Kerria, grows 4–6 feet high in an upright, rounded habit. Its pointed leaves are 3–4 inches long, doubly toothed, and deeply veined. The pure white, 1- to 2-inch flowers have 4 petals and look something like a single rose. They bloom in early spring to mid-spring. Round, shiny black berries form in fall and last throughout the winter until the shrub blooms the following spring.

GROWING TIPS

Jetbead will grow in full sun to full shade and is not fussy about soil as long as it is well drained. Remove twiggy growth at any time. Little other pruning is needed; when it is, prune after the flowers fade. Propagate new plants from cuttings or from seeds.

Currant (*Ribes*)

The genus *Ribes* includes ornamental shrubs as well as the currants and gooseberries grown for fruit. All bloom in early spring; female plants bear fruits in midsummer. Clove Currant, *R. odoratum,* is a hardy 4- to 6-foot shrub that is very decorative. The yellow flowers are very fragrant and bloom in showy, drooping, 2-inch clusters. The edible berries are smooth and black. Flowering Currant, *R. sanguineum* (pictured), grows 5–12 feet tall and is hardy in zones 6–8. The flowers are red and bloom in showy, drooping, 2- to 4-inch clusters. There are varieties with pink, deep red, and white flowers as well as double flowers. The berries are black.

GROWING TIPS

Ornamental currants are easy to grow in sun or shade in any garden soil. They can be pruned at any time. Propagate new plants from softwood or hardwood cuttings, by layering, or by stratifying seeds. Do not grow Flowering Currant in wheat-producing areas, because it is an alternate host of black stem rust.

Father Hugo's Rose *(Rosa hugonis)*

One of the first roses to bloom in the spring, Father Hugo's Rose was named for the missionary who discovered it in China. It is a 6- to 8-foot-high shrub with drooping branches that are covered with thorns. The leaves are divided into 5–13 small oval leaflets. The bright yellow flowers appear in the summer; they are single, slightly fragrant, and grow 2 inches across. The ½-inch fruits, which are called hips, are scarlet to blackish red.

Growing Tips

Plant Father Hugo's Rose in full sun. It prefers rich, moist, well-drained soil, but is one of the few roses that tolerates poor soil. It can be used as a hedge or as a background plant to lower-growing shrubs. Cut out the oldest canes each year to promote new growth; trim plants to control their size and shape after they flower. New plants can be grown from softwood or hardwood cuttings.

Rugosa Rose *(Rosa rugosa)*

Zone 3

Rugosa Rose, or Saltspray Rose, is a species (or "wild") rose that grows from 4–6 feet tall and can spread up to 10 feet across. Its leaves are deeply wrinkled and heavily veined; each leaf has 5–9 leaflets. The 3½-inch-wide flowers are usually single and pink, but there are also white, red, and double-flowered varieties. Flowers first appear in early summer and bloom all summer. The fruits, known as hips, are brick-red and 1 inch across.

GROWING TIPS

Rugosa Rose is an excellent plant for the seashore, because it grows well in pure sand and tolerates salt spray. It also makes a good barrier plant because of its dense thorns. Plant it in full sun and well-drained, acid soil. Prune Rugosa Rose at any time to remove old canes or to shape it. New plants can be grown from softwood or hardwood cuttings.

Common Pussy Willow (*Salix discolor*) Zone 3

In early spring, the fuzzy, oblong catkins of the Pussy Willow form along the branches before the leaves open. The catkins are made of flowers that have no petals or sepals but are surrounded by bracts. The narrow, 2- to 4-inch leaves are slightly toothed and are bluish green on the undersides. Mature plants can grow as much as 20 feet tall but can be kept lower in the garden by pruning. The variety 'Nana' is pictured here.

GROWING TIPS

Pussy Willow can be grown in full sun to partial shade in any garden soil, although it does best in moist soil. To force the catkins to open, cut branches in midwinter and bring them indoors. Prune Pussy Willows after they flower to shape them and control their size. Like all willows, Pussy Willow is very easy to propagate from cuttings. To assist the rooting of other plants, soak Pussy Willow cuttings in water and use the water on the other cuttings.

American Elderberry *(Sambucus canadensis)*   Zone 4

American Elderberry, a fast-growing, deciduous shrub, is cultivated for its masses of white flowers in late spring and early summer and its fruit, which is used for making wine and jelly. The plants grow 6–10 feet high and wide and have brittle branches. The leaves are divided into 7 toothed leaflets, which are 2–6 inches long. The individual flowers are tiny, but the flat-topped clusters may be up to 6 inches or more across. The tiny berries are purple to black. The variety 'Aurea' has golden-yellow leaves; 'Acutiloba' has dissected leaves.

GROWING TIPS

Plant American Elderberry in full sun or partial shade. It is easy to grow in any soil but prefers moist, well-drained sites. Because it tends to sprawl, it is well suited to an informal border. Overgrown shrubs or branches can be cut to the ground and will grow back quickly. Pinch growing tips to encourage dense growth. Propagate American Elderberry from softwood or hardwood stem cuttings or suckers.

Lavender Cotton *(Santolina chamaecyparissus)*

O ften used in herb gardens and as an edging for larger plantings, Lavender Cotton is a low, mounded, aromatic evergreen that grows rapidly to 1–2 feet high and 2–3 feet across. Its finely divided, ½-inch leaves are woolly and silvery gray. The golden-yellow, buttonlike flowers bloom in summer at the top of leafless, 6-inch stems. Because of the color of its foliage, Lavender Cotton makes a good buffer between strong colors.

GROWING TIPS

Like most gray-leaved plants, Lavender Cotton prefers dry, infertile, well-drained soil and full sun. It is very tolerant of heat and drought. Shear the plants to keep them compact after they have bloomed. If you are growing Lavender Cotton only for its foliage, you can prune it before it flowers. Start new plants from cuttings or by division in spring.

Japanese Skimmia *(Skimmia japonica)*

Japanese Skimmia is a dense, mounded, evergreen shrub. It grows 2–5 feet high and 6 feet wide and has oblong, 3- to 5-inch leaves. Small white flowers bloom in 3-inch clusters in spring. There are separate male and female plants; the flowers on the male plants are larger and are fragrant. In fall, small red berries form on the female plants and last all winter and into the following spring.

GROWING TIPS

Japanese Skimmia likes a spot in partial to full shade and moist, rich, acid soil that is well drained. It is tolerant of air pollution and grows well in cities. Be sure to plant at least 1 male plant for every 6–8 female plants if you want berries. Japanese Skimmia needs little if any pruning. Propagate new plants from seeds or from cuttings taken in fall.

Japanese Spirea *(Spiraea japonica)*

An upright deciduous shrub, Japanese Spirea grows 4–6 feet high. Its 1- to 4-inch leaves are oval to oblong and have hairs along the veins on the undersides. The tiny pink flowers bloom in early summer to midsummer in dense, flat-topped clusters that are 3 inches across. The variety *alpina,* which grows 1½–2½ feet high, makes a handsome, wide-spreading ground cover. The variety 'Little Princess' is shown here.

GROWING TIPS

Japanese Spirea is easy to grow in full sun or partial shade in a variety of soils. The most compact and floriferous growth is found in full sun and moist soil. Japanese Spirea requires little pruning, but branches can be cut to the ground if the plant becomes leggy. Any other pruning should be done in early spring. Propagate new plants from seeds or softwood cuttings.

Vanhoutte Spirea *(Spiraea × vanhouttei)*   Zone 4

In late spring, the arching branches of Vanhoutte Spirea are densely clothed in round, 1- to 2-inch clusters of white flowers. They have oval, pointed leaves that are toothed and grow 1½ inches long. The shrubs, which grow 6–8 feet high, are striking when they are allowed to grow into their full size and shape in hedges or as lawn specimens.

GROWING TIPS

Vanhoutte Spirea will tolerate partial shade but grows more densely in full sun. It will grow in any garden soil but prefers soil that is moist. It is often necessary to remove old branches to the ground; any other pruning should be done after the flowers bloom. Do not shear the plants or you will ruin their form. New plants can be propagated from stem cuttings, from seeds, or by pegging the stems to the ground and allowing them to root.

Colchis Bladdernut *(Staphylea colchica)*

Colchis Bladdernut is a deciduous shrub that grows from 8–12 feet high and has compound leaves. Each leaf has 3–5 toothed, oval, 3½-inch leaflets. The greenish-white, ¾-inch flowers are bell shaped and bloom in clusters at the ends of the branches in late spring. The curious, inflated, 2-inch seed capsules that give the plant its common name appear after the blossoms. They are showier than the flowers.

GROWING TIPS

Colchis Bladdernut prefers partial shade and moist, rich, well-drained soil. Pinch new shoots to encourage compact growth; little other pruning is needed. Colchis Bladdernut is easy to propagate from seeds or softwood cuttings.

Chinese Lilac *(Syringa × chinensis)*

There are many lilac species that deserve a place in the garden in addition to the Common Lilac *(S. vulgaris)*. One of these is Chinese Lilac, a densely branched deciduous shrub that grows to 10 feet high. The 2-inch leaves are smooth and oval with a tapering tip. The fragrant flowers are lilac to purple and bloom in 4- to 6-inch, pyramidal clusters in mid-spring to late spring. They are looser than those of Common Lilac.

Growing Tips

All lilacs grow best in full sun and well-drained soil. Fertilize them every 2 years. Remove old blossoms as soon as they fade just above the point where new buds are forming. Heavier pruning will result in the loss of next year's flowers. Prune during winter or early spring to remove all weak wood that does not bear large flower buds or that still carries the previous year's fruit. Propagate lilacs in spring from stem cuttings taken after the flowers fade.

Five-stamen Tamarisk *(Tamarix ramosissima)* Zone 3

Tamarisks are large deciduous shrubs that bear dense, wispy spikes of minute flowers at the ends of the branches in mid-spring to late spring. The flowers of Five-stamen Tamarisk are pink to rose-pink and grow in stiff, drooping spikes that are 12 inches long. The leaves are very small, only about 1/16 inch long, and completely cover the twigs, giving the plant a light, feathery effect. Five-stamen Tamarisks grow 10–15 feet high and wide.

GROWING TIPS

Tamarisks grow best in full sun and well-drained, acid soil but tolerate a wide range of soil conditions. They also tolerate salt air and grow well in sand. Prune in early spring before the buds appear. New plants can be grown from stem cuttings or from seeds.

Burkwood Viburnum
(Viburnum × burkwoodii)

Viburnums are a large genus of shrubs grown for their showy midspring flowers and the colorful berries that develop in fall. The genus includes the American Cranberry. Burkwood Viburnum is a semievergreen shrub that grows to 6 feet high. The leaves are glossy on the top but hairy underneath and have brown veins. The flowers, like those of most viburnums, are white and fragrant, blooming in 3-inch rounded clusters. They open from pink buds. Fruits, which develop in fall, are red, changing to black.

GROWING TIPS
Viburnums are easy to grow in full sun or light shade. They prefer moist, well-drained, acid soil. Prune viburnums after they flower if necessary; but pruning will remove some of the berries. Watch for and remove suckers that develop on grafted plants. Propagate by stratifying seeds, from cuttings, or by layering. For heavy berry production, plant 2 or more shrubs close together.

Lilac Chaste Tree *(Vitex agnus-castus)*

Lilac Chaste Tree is a deciduous shrub valued for its late summer bloom. Left unpruned, it can grow to 20 feet high but it is much more attractive if kept smaller. The leaves, which open late in spring, have 5–7 lance-shaped leaflets that are up to 4 inches long. They are covered with short gray hairs on the undersides and are pleasantly scented when bruised. Fragrant lavender flowers bloom in dense, narrow spikes at the tops of the branches. The cultivar 'Alba', pictured, has white flowers.

GROWING TIPS

Lilac Chaste Tree grows best in full sun but will tolerate partial shade. It grows well in any well-drained garden soil but performs best in soil that is rich, moist, and sandy. To keep the plant shapely, prune the branches to the ground early each spring or at least every other year. Propagate new plants from stem cuttings taken in summer.

Old-fashioned Weigela *(Weigela florida)*

Old-fashioned Weigela is a deciduous shrub that grows 7–10 feet high and has slightly arching, spreading branches. The elliptical, 4-inch-long leaves are hairy along the veins on the undersides. The single, funnel-shaped flowers are pale to rose-pink; they appear along the branches in late spring or early summer. There are varieties with white or dark pink flowers as well as with variegated leaves.

GROWING TIPS

Weigela grows best in full sun but will tolerate light shade. It is easy to grow in any well-drained garden soil. Prune only after the plant flowers, because flowers are produced on the growth of the previous year. Propagate new plants from stem cuttings taken in summer.

APPENDICES

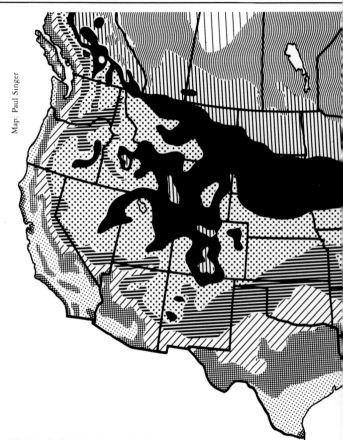

Map: Paul Singer

HARDINESS ZONE MAP

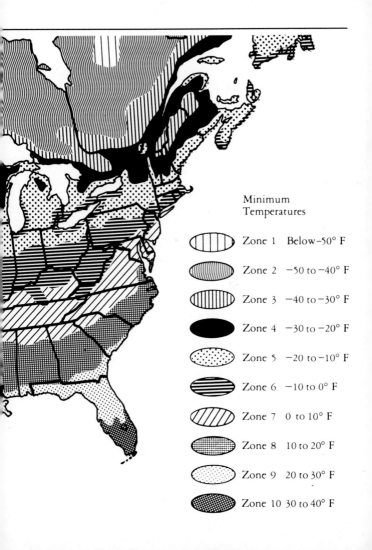

Minimum
Temperatures

Zone 1   Below –50° F

Zone 2   –50 to –40° F

Zone 3   –40 to –30° F

Zone 4   –30 to –20° F

Zone 5   –20 to –10° F

Zone 6   –10 to 0° F

Zone 7   0 to 10° F

Zone 8   10 to 20° F

Zone 9   20 to 30° F

Zone 10 30 to 40° F

GARDEN PESTS AND DISEASES

PLANT PESTS and diseases are a fact of life for a gardener. Therefore, it is helpful to become familiar with common pests and diseases in your area and to learn how to control them.

Symptoms of Plant Problems

Because the same general symptoms are associated with many diseases and pests, some experience is needed to determine their causes.

Diseases

Both fungi and bacteria are responsible for a variety of diseases ranging from leaf spots and wilts to root rot, but bacterial diseases usually make the affected plant tissues appear wetter than fungi do. Diseases caused by viruses and mycoplasma, often transmitted by aphids and leafhoppers, display such symptoms as mottled yellow or deformed leaves and twisted or stunted growth.

Insect Pests

Numerous insects attack plants. Sap-sucking insects—including aphids, leafhoppers, and scale insects—suck plant juices. The affected plant becomes yellow, stunted, and misshapen. Aphids and scale insects produce honeydew, a sticky substance that attracts ants and sooty mold fungus growth. Other pests with rasping-sucking mouthparts, such as thrips and spider mites, scrape plant tissue and then suck the juices that well up in the injured areas.

Leaf-chewers, namely beetles and caterpillars, consume plant leaves, whole or in part. Leaf miners make tunnels within the leaves, creating brown trails and causing leaf tissue to dry. In contrast, borers tunnel into shoots and stems, and their young larvae consume plant tissue, weakening the plant. Some insects, such as various grubs and maggots, feed on roots, weakening or killing the plant.

Nematodes

Microscopic roundworms called nematodes are other pests that attack roots and cause stunting and poor plant growth. Some kinds of nematodes produce galls on roots, while others produce them on leaves.

Environmental Stresses

Some types of plant illness result from environment-related stress, such as severe wind, drought, flooding, or extreme cold. Other problems are caused by salt toxicity, rodents, birds, nutritional deficiencies or excesses, pesticides, or damage from lawn mowers. Many of these injuries are avoidable if you take proper precautions.

Controlling Plant Problems

Always buy healthy disease- and insect-free shrubs, and select resistant varieties that are hardy in your area. Check leaves and canes for dead areas or off-color and stunted tissue. Give your shrubs proper care and you will avoid many problems.

Routine Preventives

By cultivating the soil routinely you will expose insects and disease-causing organisms to the sun and thus lessen their chances of surviving in your garden. In the fall, be sure to destroy infested or diseased stems, remove dead leaves and flowers, and clean up plant debris. Do not add diseased or infested material to the compost pile. Spray plants with water from time to time to dislodge insect pests and remove suffocating dust. Pick off the larger insects by hand. To discourage fungal leaf spots and blights, always water plants in the morning and allow the leaves to dry off before nightfall. For the same reason, provide adequate air circulation around leaves and stems by spacing plants properly.

Weeds provide a home for insects and diseases, so pull them up or use pre-emergent herbicides (we do not recommend the use of any other type). If you use herbicides on your lawn, do not apply them too close to shrubs or spray on a windy day. Herbicide injury may cause leaves to become elongated, strap-like, or downward-cupping.

Insecticides and Fungicides

To protect plant tissue from injury due to insects and diseases, a number of insecticides and fungicides are available. However, few products control diseases due to bacteria, viruses, and mycoplasma. Pesticides are usually either "protectant" or "systemic" in nature. Protectants keep insects or disease organisms away from uninfected foliage, while systemics move through the plant and provide some therapeutic or eradicant action as well as protection. Botanical insecticides such as pyrethrum and rotenone have a shorter residual effect on pests, but are considered less toxic and generally safer for the user and the environment than inorganic chemical insecticides. Biological control through the use of organisms like *Bacillus thuringiensis* (a bacterium toxic to moth and butterfly larvae) is effective and safe.

Recommended pesticides may vary to some extent from region to region. Consult your local Cooperative Extension Service or plant professional regarding the appropriate material to use. Always check the pesticide label to be sure that it is registered for use on the pest and plant with which you are dealing. Follow the label concerning safety precautions, dosage, and frequency of application.

GLOSSARY

Acid soil
Soil with a pH value of less than 7.

Alkaline soil
Soil with a pH value of more than 7.

Axil
The angle between a leafstalk and the stem from which it grows.

Balled and burlapped
Dug out of the ground with a ball of soil around the roots, which is tied with burlap and string for transport.

Bare-rooted
Dug out of a loose growing medium with no soil around the roots. Some shrubs are sold by nurseries in this condition.

Berry
A fleshy fruit with seeds, developed from a single ovary.

Bloom
A whitish powdery or waxy covering on some fruits.

Bract
A modified and often scalelike leaf, usually located at the base of a flower, a fruit, or a cluster of flowers or fruits.

Broad-leaved evergreen
An evergreen plant that is not a conifer.

Bud
A young and undeveloped leaf, flower, or shoot, usually covered tightly with scales.

Cane
A long, woody, pliable stem.

Capsule
A dry fruit containing more than one cell, splitting along more than one groove.

Catkin
A compact and often drooping cluster of reduced, stalkless, and usually unisexual flowers.

Compound leaf
A leaf made up of two or more leaflets.

Conifer
A cone-bearing tree or shrub, often evergreen, usually with needle-like leaves.

Container-grown
Raised in a pot that is removed before planting. Many shrubs are sold by nurseries in this form.

Corolla
Collectively, the petals of a flower.

Creeping
Prostrate or trailing over the ground or over other plants.

Crown
That part of a plant where the roots and the stem meet.

Cultivar
An unvarying plant variety maintained by vegetative propagation or by inbred seed.

Cutting
A piece of plant without roots; set in a rooting medium, it develops roots and is then potted as a new plant.

Deciduous
Dropping its leaves; not evergreen.

Dissected leaf
A deeply cut leaf, the clefts not reaching the midrib; same as a divided leaf.

Division
Propagation of a plant by separating it into two or more pieces, each of which has at least one bud and some roots.

Double-flowered
Having more than the usual number of petals, usually arranged in extra rows.

Dwarf
A plant that, due to an inherited characteristic, is shorter and/or slower-growing than normal forms.

Evergreen
Retaining green leaves for more than one annual growth cycle.

Family
A group of plants in related genera, all of which share characteristics not found in other families.

Fertile
Able to produce seed.

Fruit
The fully developed ovary of a flower, containing seeds.

Genus
A group of closely related species; plural, genera.

Germinate
To sprout, used to describe the sprouting of seeds.

Habit
The characteristic growth form or general shape of a plant.

Hardwood cutting
A cutting taken from a dormant plant after it has finished its yearly growth.

Herbaceous perennial
A plant with little or no woody tissue that dies to the ground each fall and resprouts each spring.

Horticulture
The cultivation of plants for ornament or food.

Humus
Partly or wholly decomposed vegetable matter, an important constituent of garden soil.

Hybrid
The offspring of two parent plants belonging to different species, subspecies, genera, or varieties.

Invasive
Spreading aggressively from the original site of planting.

Lance shaped
Shaped like a lance; several times longer than wide, pointed at the tip and broadest near the base.

Layering
A method of propagating plants in which a stem is pegged to the ground and covered with soil and thus induced to send out roots.

Leaflet
One of the subdivisions of a compound leaf.

Leaf mold
A type of humus consisting of partially decayed leaves.

Lime
A substance containing calcium added to soil for increased alkalinity and nutrient content.

Loam
A humus-rich soil containing up to 25 percent clay, up to 50 percent silt, and less than 50 percent sand.

Lobe
A segment of a cleft leaf or petal.

Lobed leaf
A leaf whose margin is shallowly divided.

Margin
The edge of a leaf.

Mulch
A protective covering spread over the soil around the base of plants to retard evaporation, control temperature, or suppress weeds.

Neutral soil
Soil that is neither acid nor alkaline, having a pH value of 7.

Node
The place on a stem where leaves or branches are attached.

Opposite
Arranged along a twig or shoot in pairs, with one on each side.

Ovate
Oval, with the broader end at the base.

Panicle
A compound, branching flower cluster, blooming from bottom to top, and never terminating in a flower.

Peat moss
Partly decomposed moss, rich in nutrients and with a high water retention, used as a component of garden soil.

Perennial
A plant whose life spans several growing seasons and that produces seeds in several growing seasons, rather than only one.

Petal
One of a series of flower parts lying within the sepals and outside the stamens and pistils, often large and brightly colored.

pH
A symbol for the hydrogen ion content of the soil, and thus a means of expressing the acidity or alkalinity of the soil.

Pistil
The female reproductive organ of a flower.

Pod
A dry, one-celled fruit, with thicker walls than a capsule.

Pollen
Minute grains containing the male germ cells and produced by the stamens.

Propagate
To produce new plants, either by vegetative means involving the rooting of pieces of a plant, or by sowing seeds.

Prostrate
Lying on the ground; creeping.

Prune
To cut the branches of a woody plant to spur growth, maintain vigor, or shape the plant.

Raceme
A long flower cluster on which individual flowers are borne on small stalks from a common, larger, central stalk.

Rhizome
A horizontal stem at or just below the surface of the ground, distinguished from a root by the presence of nodes.

Rock garden
A landscape created with rocks and plants native to cliffs and mountainous regions.

Runner
A prostrate shoot, rooting at its nodes.

Scarified seeds
Seeds that have been scratched or sanded in order to induce them to absorb water and germinate.

Screen
A single plant or grouping of plants used to bar certain parts of the landscape from view.

Seed
A fertilized, ripened ovule, almost always covered with a protective coating and contained in a fruit.

Semievergreen
Retaining at least some green foliage well into winter, or shedding leaves only in cold climates.

Sepal
One of the outermost series of flower parts, arranged in a ring outside the petals, and usually green and leaflike.

Shrub border
A row of shrubs, usually of mixed species, allowed to grow naturally.

Simple leaf
A leaf with an undivided blade; not compound or composed of leaflets.

Softwood
Immature stems of woody plants.

Species
A population of plants or animals whose members reproduce by breeding with each other, but which is reproductively isolated from other populations.

Specimen
A plant placed conspicuously alone, usually in a prominent place, so as to show off its ornamental qualities.

Spike
An elongated flower cluster whose flowers are stalkless.

Spine
A strong, sharp, usually woody projection from the stem or branches of a plant.

Spreading plant
A plant whose branches grow more or less horizontally.

Stamen
The male reproductive organ of a flower.

Sterile
Incapable of producing seeds, either because of a lack of stamens and pistils or because of internal genetic incompatibilities.

Stolon
A horizontal stem growing along or just under the ground from the top of which a new plant arises; a runner or unthickened rhizome.

Stone
A single seed surrounded by a hard shell and covered by pulp.

Stratify
To keep seeds under cool, dark, moist conditions in order to encourage them to break dormancy after this treatment.

Subshrub
A partly woody plant whose stems die back partially in fall.

Succulent
A plant with thick, fleshy leaves or stems that contain abundant water-storage tissue.

Sucker
A secondary shoot arising from underground buds on the roots of a plant.

Terminal
Borne at the tip of a stem or shoot, rather than in the axil.

Thorn
A short, sharp, woody outgrowth of a stem.

Toothed
Having the margin divided into small, toothlike segments.

Topiary
The art of shearing trees and shrubs into unusual shapes.

Tuber
A swollen, mostly underground stem that bears buds and serves as a storage site for food.

Variegated
Marked, striped, or blotched with some color other than green.

Variety
A population of plants differing slightly but consistently from the typical form of the species, and occurring naturally. Also loosely applied to forms produced in cultivation.

Weeping
Having drooping branches.

Woody
Producing hard rather than fleshy stems and having buds that survive above ground in winter.

PHOTO CREDITS

Ruth Allen, 78

Gillian Beckett, 37

Al Bussewitz, PHOTO/NATS ©, 38, 66, 82

Thomas E. Eltzroth, 28

Derek Fell, 29, 49, 61, 62, 67, 81, 86, 88, 99, 104

Charles Marden Fitch, 43, 56, 87

Judy Glattstein, 92

Pamela J. Harper, 26, 30, 32, 33, 35, 39, 40, 41, 42, 44, 48, 50, 51, 55, 58, 64, 68, 71, 79, 80, 83, 85, 89, 93, 95, 97

Walter H. Hodge, 59, 69, 74, 77, 84, 90, 96, 103

Dorothy S. Long, PHOTO/NATS ©, Cover

John J. Smith, PHOTO/NATS ©, 2, 25, 70

Joy Spurr, 27, 63

Steven M. Still, 34, 36, 45, 47, 54, 57, 60, 65, 72, 73, 75, 94, 101, 102

David M. Stone, PHOTO/NATS ©, 53

George Taloumis, 31, 52, 76, 91, 98, 100

Doug Wechsler, 46

INDEX

Abelia, 26
 Glossy, 26
Abelia. 26
 'Edward Goucher', 26
 × *grandiflora.* 26
Abelialeaf, Korean, 27
Abeliophyllum distichum. 27
Acacia longifolia. 28
Aesculus parviflora. 29
Alder, Spiked, 43
Almond, Dwarf Flowering, 86
Amelanchier stolonifera. 30
Andromeda, 83
Aronia. 31
 arbutifolia. 31
 melanocarpa. 31
Azalea, Exbury Hybrid, 87

Baccharis halimifolia. 32
Beauty Bush, 70
Bladdernut, Colchis, 99
Bluebeard, 37
Broom
 Easter, 49
 Scotch, 49
 Warminster, 49
Buckeye, Bottlebrush, 29
Buddleia. 33
 alternifolia. 33
 davidii. 33

Butterfly Bush, 33
 Alternate Leaf, 33
 Orange-eye, 33
Button Bush, 39

Calluna
 vulgaris. 34
 vulgaris 'Million', 34
Camellia, 35
 Japanese, 35
 Sasanqua, 35
Camellia. 35
 japonica. 35
 sasanqua. 35
 sasanqua 'Showa No Sakae', 35
Caragana arborescens. 36
Carmel Creeper, 38
Caryopteris
 × *clandonensis.* 37
 × *clandonensis* 'Blue Mist', 37
 × *clandonensis* 'Kew Blue', 37
Ceanothus, 38
 Inland, 38
 San Diego, 38
Ceanothus. 38
 cyaneus. 38
 griseus var. *horizontalis.* 38
 ovatus. 38
Cephalanthus occidentalis. 39
Cercis chinensis. 40

Chaenomeles, 41
  japonica, 41
  speciosa, 41
  speciosa 'Phylis Moore', 41
Chaste Tree, Lilac, 103
Chokeberry, 31
  Black, 31
  Red, 31
Cinquefoil, Shrubby, 85
Cistus, 42
  × *hybridus*, 42
  ladanifer, 42
  × *purpureus*, 42
Clethra, Summersweet, 43
Clethra
  alnifolia, 43
  alnifolia 'Pink Spires', 43
Colutea arborescens, 44
Cornus racemosa, 45
Corylopsis, 46
  glabrescens, 46
  pauciflora, 46
Cotinus coggygria, 47
Cotoneaster, 48
  Bearberry, 48
  Cranberry, 48
  Creeping, 48
  Spreading, 48
Cotoneaster, 48
  adpressus, 48
  apiculatus, 48
  dammeri, 48
  dammeri 'Skogsholm', 48
  divaricatus, 48
Cranberry, American, 102

Cream Bush, 63
Currant, 90
  Clove, 90
  Flowering, 90
Cytisus
  × *praecox*, 49
  racemosus, 49
  scoparius, 49
  scoparius 'Goldfinch', 49

Daphne, 50
  Burkwood, 50
  Fragrant, 50
  Rose, 50
  Winter, 50
Daphne, 50
  × *burkwoodii*, 50
  × *burkwoodii* 'Somerset', 50
  cneorum, 50
  odora, 50
Deutzia, 51
  Fuzzy, 51
  Slender, 51
Deutzia, 51
  gracilis, 51
  scabra, 51
  scabra 'Candidissima', 51
Dirca palustris, 52
Dogwood, Gray, 45

Elderberry, American, 94
Enkianthus, Redvein, 53
Enkianthus campanulatus, 53
Erica × *darleyensis*, 54
Exochorda, 55

× *macrantha*. 55
× *macrantha* 'The Bride', 55
racemosa. 55

Forsythia, 56
  Border, 56
  Weeping, 56
Forsythia. 56
  × *intermedia*. 56
  suspensa var. *sieboldii*. 56
Fothergilla, Dwarf, 57
Fothergilla
  gardenii. 57
  major. 57

Gardenia, 58
Gardenia jasminoides. 58
Gaylussacia brachycera. 59
Genista. 60
  lydia. 60
  tinctoria. 60
Grape Holly, Oregon, 77
Greenweed, Dyer's, 60
Groundsel Bush, 32

Hamamelis. 61
  × *intermedia*. 61
  mollis. 61
  mollis 'Brevipetala', 61
  virginiana. 61
Heath, Darley, 54
Heather, Scotch, 34
Hibiscus
  syriacus. 62
  syriacus 'Althea', 62

Holodiscus discolor. 63
Honeysuckle
  Amur, 73
  Tatarian, 73
  Winter, 73
Huckleberry, Box, 59
Hydrangea, 64
  Bigleaf, 64
  Oakleaf, 64
  Panicle, 64
  Smooth, 64
Hydrangea. 64
  arborescens. 64
  macrophylla. 64
  paniculata. 64
  paniculata 'Grandiflora', 64
  quercifolia. 64
Hypericum. 65
  calycinum. 65
  frondosum. 65

Itea virginica. 66

Jasmine
  Cape, 58
  Winter, 67
Jasminum nudiflorum. 67
Jetbead, 89
Juniper Berry, 59

Kalmia. 68
  angustifolia. 68
  latifolia. 68
Kerria
  Japanese, 69

White, 89
Kerria
  japonica. 69
  japonica 'Pleniflora', 69
Kolkwitzia amabilis. 70

Laurel, 68
  Mountain, 68
  Sheep, 68
Lavender Cotton, 95
Leatherwood, 52
Leucothoe, 71
  Coast, 71
  Drooping, 71
Leucothoe. 71
  axillaris. 71
  fontanesiana. 71
Ligustrum. 72
  amurense. 72
  japonicum. 72
  obtusifolium. 72
  obtusifolium var. *regelianum*. 72
Lilac
  Chinese, 100
  Common, 100
Lonicera
  fragrantissima. 73
  maackii. 73
  tatarica. 73
Loropetalum, 74
Loropetalum chinense. 74

Magnolia
  Lily, 75
  Star, 76

Magnolia
  quinquepeta. 75
  stellata. 76
Mahonia, 77
  Leatherleaf, 77
Mahonia. 77
  aquifolium. 77
  bealei. 77
Mock-Orange
  Common, 80
  Lemoine, 80
  Sweet, 80
  Virginal, 80

Nerium oleander. 78
Ninebark
  Common, 82
  Goldleaf, 82

Oleander, 78
Orange
  Hardy, 84
  Trifoliate, 84
Osmanthus
  Fortune's, 79
  Holly, 79
Osmanthus
  × *fortunei*. 79
  fragrans. 79
  heterophyllus. 79
  heterophyllus 'Myrtifolius', 79

Pea Shrub, Siberian, 36
Pearlbush, 55
  Common, 55

Pepperbush, Sweet, 43
Philadelphus
  coronarius. 80
  × *lemoinei*. 80
  × *virginalis*. 80
Phlomis fruticosa. 81
Physocarpus
  opulifolius. 82
  opulifolius 'Luteus', 82
Pieris, 83
  Japanese, 83
  Mountain, 83
Pieris. 83
  floribunda. 83
  japonica. 83
  japonica 'Wada', 83
Poncirus trifoliata. 84
Potentilla fruticosa. 85
Privet, 72
  Amur, 72
  Border, 72
  Hedge, 72
  Japanese, 72
  Regel's, 72
Prunus glandulosa. 86
Pussy Willow, Common, 93

Quince
  Common Flowering, 41
  Japanese, 41

Redbud, Chinese, 40
Rhododendron, Yako, 88
Rhododendron
  'Aurora', 87

Exbury, 87
  yakusimanum. 88
Rhodotypos scandens. 89
Ribes. 90
  odoratum. 90
  sanguineum. 90
Rockrose, 42
  Crimson-spot, 42
  Orchid, 42
  White, 42
Rope Bark, 52
Rosa
  hugonis. 91
  rugosa. 92
Rose
  Father Hugo's, 91
  Rugosa, 92
  Saltspray, 92
Rose-of-Sharon, 62

Sage, Jerusalem, 81
St. Johnswort, 65
  Aaronsbeard, 65
  Golden, 65
Salix
  discolor. 93
  discolor 'Nana', 93
Sambucus
  canadensis. 94
  canadensis 'Acutiloba', 94
  canadensis 'Aurea', 94
Santolina chamaecyparissus. 95
Senna, Common Bladder, 44
Serviceberry, Running, 30
Skimmia, Japanese, 96

Skimmia japonica. 96
Smoke Tree, 47
Smokebush, 47
Spiraea
  japonica. 97
  japonica var. *alpina.* 97
  japonica 'Little Princess', 97
  × *vanhouttei.* 98
Spirea
  Blue, 37
  Japanese, 97
  Vanhoutte, 98
Staphylea colchica. 99
Sweet Spire, Virginia, 66
Syringa
  × *chinensis.* 100
  vulgaris. 100

Tamarisk, Five-stamen, 101
Tamarix ramosissima. 101

Tea Olive, Fragrant, 79

Viburnum, Burkwood, 102
Viburnum × *burkwoodii.* 102
Vitex
  agnus-castus. 103
  agnus-castus 'Alba', 103

Wattle, Golden, 28
Weigela, Old-fashioned, 104
Weigela florida. 104
Winter Hazel, 46
  Buttercup, 46
  Fragrant, 46
Witch Hazel, 61
  Chinese, 61
  Common, 61
  Hybrid, 61
Woodwaxen, 60
  Lydia, 60

CHANTICLEER PRESS
STEWART, TABORI & CHANG

Publisher
ANDREW STEWART

Senior Editor
ANN WHITMAN

Editor
CAROL MCKEOWN

Project Editor
AMY HUGHES

Production
KATHY ROSENBLOOM
KARYN SLUTSKY

Design
JOSEPH RUTT